THE GREAT WALL

From Beginning to End

THE GREAT WALL

From Beginning to End

Photography by **MICHAEL YAMASHITA**

Text by **MICHAEL YAMASHITA** *and* **WILLIAM LINDESAY**

STERLING

New York / London

www.sterlingpublishing.com

Cover: Jinshanling Wall, part of the Wild Wall.
Page ii: Jinshanling Wall in late afternoon.
Pages vi–vii: Badaling Wall battlement.

— To Lil and Maggie, with love —

STERLING and the distinctive Sterling logo are registered trademarks of
Sterling Publishing Co., Inc.

Library of Congress Cataloging-in-Publication Data Available

10 9 8 7 6 5 4 3 2 1

Published by Sterling Publishing Co., Inc.
387 Park Avenue South, New York, NY 10016

Distributed in Canada by Sterling Publishing
c/o Canadian Manda Group, 165 Dufferin Street
Toronto, Ontario, Canada M6K 3H6
Distributed in the United Kingdom by GMC Distribution Services
Castle Place, 166 High Street, Lewes, East Sussex, England BN7 1XU
Distributed in Australia by Capricorn Link (Australia) Pty. Ltd.
P.O. Box 704, Windsor, NSW 2756, Australia

Photos © 2007 by Michael Yamashita
Text © 2007 by Michael Yamashita and William Lindesay

Book design and layout: Christopher Cannon, Eric Baker Design Associates
Maps: XNR Productions
Chinese Calligraphy: Rita Chen

Sterling ISBN-13: 978-1-4027-3160-0
        ISBN-10: 1-4027-3160-4

For information about custom editions, special sales, premium and
corporate purchases, please contact Sterling Special Sales
Department at 800-805-5489 or specialsales@sterlingpublishing.com.

ACKNOWLEDGMENTS

I gratefully acknowledge the *National Geographic* magazine, for whom I have been shooting for twenty-eight years, whose support made this book possible. Thanks to former editor-in-chief Bill Allen and current editor-in-chief Chris Johns; to former director of photography, and my travel companion to the North Korean border, Kent Kobersteen, and to deputy director of photography Susan Smith; to David Whitmore for his excellent thirty-page magazine layout for the January 2003 *National Geographic* magazine story on the Wall, with special thanks to picture editor Elizabeth Krist for her good guidance and picture choices for both the magazine story and this book.

I was very fortunate to be paired with writer Peter Hessler, whose good humor and insightful knowledge of the Wall, of China, and of the Chinese kept everything in perspective. My fixers, Jia Liming and Matthew Hu, were world-class travelers who made the miles go quickly. Our driver, Yang Xiaoji, got us there fast and safe. Thanks to Ciao Ming and Zhao Yang of the Beijing Cultural Development Foundation, our local sponsors, and to China's Wall experts, Lao Zhewen of the Cultural Heritage Bureau and Liu Yijiang, who traveled with me in Lijiang, Shanxi, and Inner Mongolia.

I would also like to acknowledge William Lindesay, the only other person I know, besides Pete Hessler and me, who has traveled the full length of the Wall. He and his group, the International Friends of the Wall, deserve special thanks for their good work in preserving and protecting this monument for the world.

Thanks to my agent, Mike Shatzkin, and to Martha Moran, and to my wife, Elizabeth Bibb, my personal editor-in-chief, as well as to my studio manager, Julie Qualmann, who helps put out fires, both home and abroad. Much appreciation to designer Christopher Cannon of Eric Baker Design Associates and to the entire team at Sterling Publishing, including Jo Fagan, Rebecca Maines, Karen Nelson, Edwin Kuo, Christine Kwasnik, Rebecca Cremonese, and Fred Dubose, and to Sterling publisher Charles Nurnberg for his enthusiasm for this project.

— MICHAEL YAMASHITA

TABLE OF CONTENTS

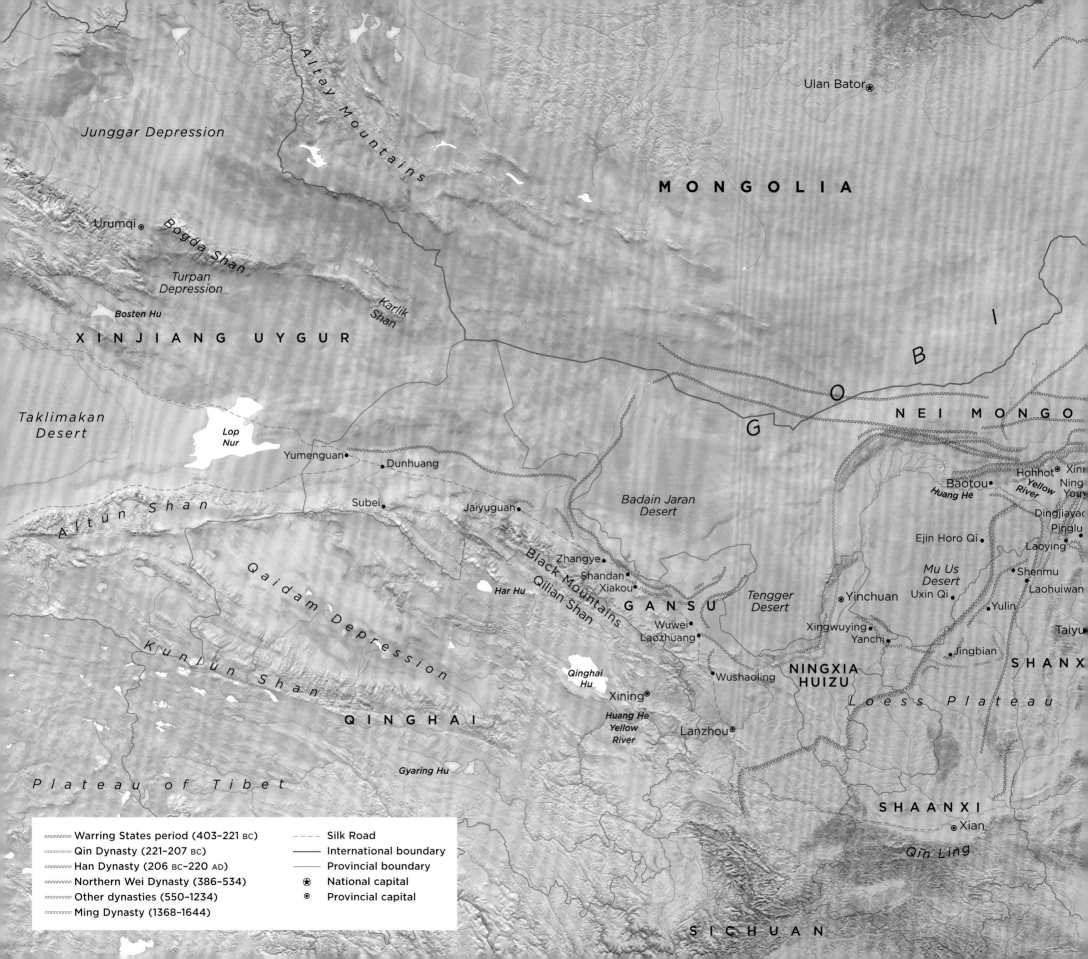

Junggar Depression

Altay Mountains

Ulan Bator

MONGOLIA

Urumqi
Bogda Shan
Turpan Depression
Karlik Shan

XINJIANG UYGUR
Bosten Hu

G O B I

Taklimakan Desert

Lop Nur

G O B

NEI MONGO

Yumenguan
Dunhuang
Altun Shan
Subei
Jaiyuguan

Badain Jaran Desert

Hohhot   Xin
Baotou   Ning
Huang He   You
Yellow
River

Dingjiaya
Pinglu
Laoying

Qaidam Depression

Black Mountains
Zhangye
Shandan
Har Hu   Xiakou
Qilian Shan

GANSU

Tengger Desert

Ejin Horo Qi

Mu Us
Desert
Shenmu
Uxin Qi   Laohuiwan

Kunlun Shan

Wuwei
Laozhuang

Yinchuan

Yulin

Qinghai
Hu

Xining

Xingwuying

Yanchi

Taiyu

Jingbian

SHANX

QINGHAI

Wushaoling

NINGXIA
HUIZU

Loess Plateau

Huang He
Yellow
River
Lanzhou

Gyaring Hu

Plateau of Tibet

SHAANXI

Xian

Qin Ling

	Warring States period (403–221 BC)		Silk Road
	Qin Dynasty (221–207 BC)		International boundary
	Han Dynasty (206 BC–220 AD)		Provincial boundary
	Northern Wei Dynasty (386–534)	✴	National capital
	Other dynasties (550–1234)	◉	Provincial capital
	Ming Dynasty (1368–1644)		

S I C H U A N

HEILONGJIANG

Harbin

JILIN

Changchun

LIAONING

Shenyang

NORTH KOREA

Dandong

Simatai

Huangyaguan Reservoir

Jiankou   Panjiakou

eshengbu   Badaling

Shanhaiguan

Pyongyang

chenchuanbu   Juyongguan

Datong   Beijing   HEBEI

gciyao   BEIJING

TIANJIN

Tianjin

Bo Hai

HEBEI

Seoul

Shijiazhuang

SOUTH KOREA

Grand Canal

Jinan

Yellow Sea

SHANDONG

Yellow River
Huang He

Grand Canal

ngzhou

HENAN   Huaiyin

JIANGSU

ANHUI

Hefei   Nanjing

Shanghai

0   100   200 miles

0   100   200 kilometers

RUSSIA

KAZAKHSTAN

MONGOLIA

N. KOREA

CHINA

S. KOREA

East China Sea

INDIA

Bay of Bengal

South China Sea

Area of detail

Wichita   Washington, D.C.

Ming Wall size comparison

PREFACE

In Search of the Real Wall
by Michael Yamashita

THE GREAT WALL IS GENERALLY THE FIRST PLACE outside Beijing that tourists visit, and it is usually the highlight and most memorable part of everyone's trip to China. It certainly was for me. As an Asia specialist and photographer working for *National Geographic* magazine for twenty-five years, I've visited the Great Wall many times since my first trip on assignment to China in 1982. On subsequent assignments, as I photographed other sections of the Wall across northern China (particularly along the Silk Road in Gansu), I developed a wondrous appreciation for the length and breadth of its geography as it snakes its way through the landscape. I knew after that first trip that it was only a matter of time before I would propose a story on the Wall to my editors at *National Geographic*. Twenty years after my first visit, I decided the time was right.

My proposal was littered with what I later learned were many Wall myths and misconceptions: *The volume of its building material is greater than all that used in Britain's building at that time . . . A continuous wall built by the Qin is a single system serving to keep out marauding bands of nomads and to communicate with the capital, Xian . . . Over two thousand years old, the world's oldest construction project . . .*

I discovered there's virtually no limit to the misinformation out there about the Wall. As it turns out, much of that misinformation came from the only other story *National Geographic* had published on the Wall, which appeared in the February 1923 issue, entitled "A Thousand Miles Along the Great Wall of China." The story led with the most widely believed myth about the Wall . . . *"the only work of man's hands which would be visible to the human eye from the moon is the Great Wall of China."* That assertion, as we all now know, proved false as we entered the space age.

My story proposal nevertheless passed muster. The assignment was simple: Follow the Great Wall from its beginning at the North Korean border to its end in the Taklilmakhan desert and meet the people whose ancestors built and defended the Wall. So I began my personal journey in the fall of 2001, in search of the *real* Great Wall.

The writer assigned to the story was Beijing-based *New Yorker* correspondent and best-selling author Peter Hessler. I loved his book *Rivertown* for its insight and understanding of today's China and Chinese, as viewed from the perspective of a small down-river village far from the mainstream. Although we didn't travel together (writers and photographers do very different jobs), our regular exchanges about interesting locations, experiences, and people met along the way were invaluable. We became fast friends as fellow travelers often do, having shared a unique journey.

The greatest thing about the Wall, whose length is roughly equivalent to the distance from Washington, D.C., to Wichita, Kansas, is the geography of the lands it travels through. Once marking the northernmost frontier of the Empire, it now runs through the heart of peasant China. Here lie the poorest regions, where the climate is at its harshest, where rainfall is rare and the ground is hard, where the desert meets the cultivated soil. This is the China least reported on, the China least touched by today's economic revolution. It is this China that I find most compelling for pictures—the traditional China that is fast disappearing, the China I fell in love with when I first visited in 1982.

In the spirit of "if you build it, they will come," a man starts work on a Great Wall billboard in the desert near Dunhuang.

INTRODUCTION

by William Lindesay

I FIRST BECAME FASCINATED BY THE GREAT WALL during my boyhood in Lancashire, when I saw the Wall depicted on a map of China in my school atlas. In fact, I vowed that someday I would walk its entire length. Nearly twenty years later, a visit to Hadrian's Wall, the Roman-built structure in the north of England, rekindled my desire to set off on that Eastern journey of discovery. Finally, in 1986, I set foot on the Great Wall for the first time—and I have been there ever since.

The wall of which I speak was built by the Ming Dynasty (1368–1644 AD)—like earlier walls, intended to defend China from the nomads of the northern steppe. In walking from one end of the Ming Wall to the other and subsequently settling within its shadow I have become familiar with the smallest details of the fabled structure and its attendant gates, beacon towers, fortresses, barracks, commanderies, arsenals, granaries, and fortified towns. Yet the more I walk of the Wall and the more I see, the more I learn—and the greater the Wall becomes.

Hadrian's Wall, in the north of England, spanned 78 miles (126 kilometers).

Winding through the mountains north of Beijing and to points east and west, this crenellated stone structure is the culmination of more than 1,200 years of Chinese wall-building. Earlier walls were earthen ramparts reinforced by gravel and reeds, and most stood farther north. It is believed that in a few places the Ming built upon the remains of the walls of the Northern Qi Dynasty (550–577 AD), some sections of which the Sui (581–618 AD) repaired or replaced. But the belief that Ming wall-builders used the first "great wall" as a foundation is a misconception: the Qin Wall—begun by China's first emperor around 215 BC—stood almost a hundred kilometers north of the line the Ming Wall would follow, as did the wall of the Han Dynasty (206 BC–8 AD).

For better or worse, "Great Wall" has become a collective term for the defensive walls built by the Qin, Han, Northern Qi, Sui, and Ming. (The defenses were called "border walls" or "long walls" by the Chinese to distinguish them from the walls encircling cities.) Many Chinese dynasties built no border walls at all—not least because six of the thirty or so dynasties that rose and fell between 1025 BC and 1644 AD were ruled by the northern invaders whom the walls were intended to keep out.

The construction of China's wall system was marked by turbulence from the beginning, when the Qin Wall rose at great human cost. The fervency—indeed, ruthlessness—of some of the wall-building early emperors harked back to the first emperor's certainty that walls were necessary for maintaining Chinese security, no matter how much blood, sweat, tears, and treasure it took to erect them.

The pressure to work at a frenzied pace at some sites, combined with the inevitable injuries caused by hard labor, resulted in untold numbers of deaths. Little wonder the collective Great Wall has been called "the world's largest cemetery." Legend tells of Meng Jiang-nu, wife of a forced laborer on the Wall at Shanhaiguan, who went to the Wall to bring her husband winter clothes but arrived to find he had already expired from the cold. Her tears caused the Wall to open, revealing the bones of thousands of workers who had died there. She reburied them, then killed herself.

In the days of the Qin, Han, Northern Qi, and Sui, many workers' lives was a price government officials were willing to pay to keep the Chinese safe from neighbors they knew as barbarians.

The views of historians on the usefulness of the walls range across the board. Among the opinions expressed in books and academic treatises are those holding that the walls ultimately failed to keep invaders at bay because of poor planning and design; that, from a political standpoint, the walls were built as much to keep the Chinese in as the invaders out; and that massive wall-building projects by the Ming were meant to keep the army occupied and thus minimize the chances of military rebellion.

What is not in dispute is the level of engineering ingenuity it took to erect the Ming Wall—the length of which is hard to pin down but is generally said to be around 6,770 kilometers (4,200 miles). Builders routed it across deserts, over entire mountain ranges, and directly over peaks. They built its ramparts up inclines where it was difficult enough to even stand, constructing it as a contour by making it cling to precipitous slopes as if by roots—all at a time when the tools of the wall-building trade were rudimentary.

During the Ming Dynasty, the soldiers who largely built the Wall were paid for their efforts. If any laborers were enlisted, it is doubtful that they were ever subjected to the harsh treatment suffered by the corvèe laborers of earlier dynasties. The benign treatment of the labor force, advanced construction techniques, and stronger building materials—in particular, brick and stone—set the Ming miles apart from their wall-building predecessors.

A PHOTOGRAPHER'S ADVENTURES

In February 1923, *National Geographic* published an article titled "A Thousand Miles Along the Great Wall of China." The thirty-two-page story led off with, "The only work of man's hands which would be visible to the human eye from the moon is the Great Wall of China." This dubious

China's first astronaut, Yang Liwei, went into space in 2003 where he tested the theory that the Great Wall would be visible from space. He found that it was not.

assertion of long standing was quashed in the era of space exploration. The larger significance of the *National Geographic* article was its introduction of the Great Wall to the public of the world at large.

More than eight decades after the article appeared, the assignment for *National Geographic* photographer Michael Yamashita was to follow the Great Wall constructions from their beginning at the North Korean border to their end in the deserts of the west. In the process he was to meet and photograph the people whose ancestors built and defended the Wall.

Now, Yamashita recounts in lively fashion what he observed while shooting the Ming Wall and the remains of the Han Wall for the *National Geographic* article (January 2003 issue). He tells us not only what has become of the walls but also reveals their human side—in particular, the villagers whose lives revolve around the Ming Wall, the feelings people have for it, and the Wall's inevitable commercialization. Also found in each chapter is my brief history respectively portraying the five primary wall-building dynasties and their emperors, some of whose stories seem stranger than fiction.

The history accompanying Chapter 4 (Beijing: The Tourist Wall) is a review of how the Ming Wall has fared in the last century—which brings me back to my relationship with the Wall. I trained my "feet-on" focus on the Wall for eleven years before I realized that serious conservation efforts were in order. It was clear that the first item on the agenda was the elimination of the garbage and graffiti despoiling certain wall sections. The next step, in 1998, was to organize the first public cleanup of the Great Wall, which saw one hundred twenty volunteers armed with government-supplied rubbish bins combing the Jinshanling section on October 1—the National Day marking the birth of the People's Republic of China. The next year, volunteers recruited by thirty-five foreign embassies in Beijing participated in the cleanup campaign. Then, in 2001, I founded International Friends of the Wall. Today the activities of this nonprofit organization range from raising public consciousness of the Wall's endangered status to spearheading volunteer efforts to soliciting corporate funding for wall repairs.

In both picture and word, *The Great Wall* casts a new light on a manmade structure that, since its completion, has not been—and probably never will be—exceeded in terms of its scale and audacity. With Michael's journey along the length of the Wall, and mine through its history, we attempt herein to capture the Ming and Han walls of today, from the border of North Korea to the deserts of the west, and to take you on an enlightening and entertaining armchair journey of your own.

WILLIAM LINDESAY
Founder, International Friends of the Wall

Opposite: A Bactrian camel takes a break from plowing beside remains of the Han Wall, built to protect the trade corridor known as the Silk Road. Dust from the Gobi Desert gives the sky its yellow cast.

Above: The legend of Meng Jiang-nu, whose tears at the death of her husband opened the Wall and revealed how many others had died in its making, is depicted in this early twentieth-century print.

ONE

IN SIGHT OF NORTH KOREA

— — — — — — —

A Glimpse of the Han Wall

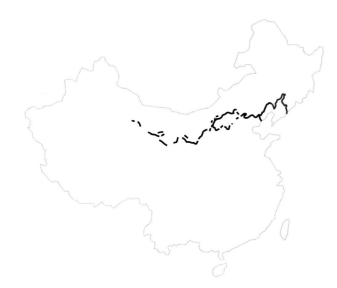

長
城

Previous page: The train running from Beijing to Dandong follows the route of the Ming Wall. Shown here is the hard-seat sleeping car.

I BEGAN MY JOURNEY OF DISCOVERY OF THE GREAT WALL at (fittingly enough) the Great Wall Hotel in Beijing, where I and my traveling companion—Kent Kobersteen, who at the time was director of photography at *National Geographic* magazine—met our guide, historian and Wall expert Liu Yijiang. The next day, the three of us headed northeast by train to Liaoning Province and the city of Dandong, which sits on the banks of the river that forms the border between China and North Korea: the Yalu. Here is found the Great Wall's easternmost point, a section of the Han Wall which may or may not have been reconstructed by the Ming. It is either the beginning or the end of the collective Great Wall, depending on the direction you travel.

We had decided to take the train rather than fly to Dandong because stretches of the railroad tracks follow the route of the Ming Wall and I hoped we might glimpse some section of it during the long overnight journey. Having photographed many major stories about China for *National Geographic* from the early nineties on, I was proud to be showing Kent the ropes on his first trip to China. Part of Kent's job was to stay in touch with photographers and how they work in the field, as well as to familiarize himself with the problems and difficulties we face in various countries and regions, by accompanying us on the road.

After settling in for the long ride in the "soft seat section," we made our way to the dining car. The flat landscape of Hebei Province hurtled past the window in the rose tones of sunset, with no Wall in sight. We ordered a few beers to go along with a set menu of rice, a meat, a vegetable, and soup. Kent, who stands six feet two inches and weighs two hundred fifty pounds

Food vendors cater to the large community of North Koreans in Baoshan, in Liaoning province's Kuandian county. From their tents the peddlers serve up a range of Korean snacks, rice wine, and beer.

Overleaf: Outside the city of Dandong, workers use Ming techniques and materials to erect the all-new Tiger Mountain Great Wall, which runs along the China–North Korea border, the Yalu River.

(and has a large personality, voice, and appetite to match), admired both the taste and the label of his first Chinese beer other than the ubiquitous Tsing Tao. Our dining car attendant offered to peel off the label for Kent to keep as a memento, and then soaked the bottle in hot water until the label loosened and slipped off. That night we collected three of these trophies (a label from each of the three provinces we traveled through—Hebei, a bit of Inner Mongolia, and Liaoning), and what we dubbed "the label game" became a genial diversion for the entire trip.

We arrived in Dandong at dawn, packing off to our hotel for a breakfast of rice porridge, pickles, a hard-boiled egg, and kimchi (Korea's national dish). We then headed to the Yalu River for a close-up look at North Korea.

Stopping a mere hundred yards from the North Korean side of the river, we shot pictures of ourselves on the broken bridge called the "bridge to nowhere," complete with a bombshell bearing a sign in Chinese: TAKE PHOTOGRAPH HERE. Chinese tourists dutifully lined up to comply, some paying extra to dress up in North Korean Army uniforms and hold toy guns for their group pictures. This bridge, built by the Japanese, was destroyed by U.S. planes during the Korean War. It stops exactly at mid-river at the border. A brand-new bridge runs alongside, with traffic heading pretty much one way into North Korea.

We had boarded a speedboat and set off for a closer look at the north side of the border when we were told, "No pictures, please." While this is usually the worst thing for a photographer to hear, there was nothing to see from water level, thanks to a large berm above the riverbank.

Next came lunch in a floating restaurant boat offering up Korean food served by North Korean waitresses. We learned that the waitresses were part of a large Korean community of some one hundred fifty Korean families who have lived in China since 1981—all of them refugees who escaped the iron-fisted regime to the north.

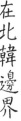

在北韓邊界

North Korean women in traditional dress brighten the village of Baoshan as they perform a dance during a festival celebrating Dan Noze, North Korea's most important holiday.

HAPPENING UPON A FESTIVAL

After collecting another batch of Korean beer labels, we headed to the Korean area of Kuandian—where, as our photographer's luck would have it, the locals were celebrating Dan Noze, North Koreans' most important festival. At the Korean school, the festival was in full swing. The entire community had turned out in traditional costume to dance, eat Korean food, and play Korean games. My favorite game to watch was the grandmothers' relay race, in which five groups of elderly women were handed plates of food that they then balanced on their heads (as is customary in the old country) while they ran a hundred-foot course. The first to cross the finish line without dropping her plate was the winner.

That evening, Kent was in fine form as our hosts decided to challenge us to a friendly game of beer drinking, as they often do with foreign guests. Normally I would beg off, knowing better than to get into a contest where the only prize is a major headache the next morning. But this time, knowing that Kent was a ringer who could bring the challengers to their knees, I encouraged the match.

We had not even gotten our first plate of peanuts before glasses were filled for a *gambei*, the bottoms-up toast to our Korean good fortune. It had been a long day, warm for May that far north, and we all were thirsty. Chinese drinking glasses are about the size of American juice glasses (i.e., small), so each time Kent's was filled he downed the beer and slammed the glass on the table for a refill, mainly to quench his thirst.

Our Chinese hosts, unaccustomed to foreigners taking the lead, were forced to follow suit. After nine or ten rounds, our hosts sheepishly called off the contest in fear of the consequences if they continued. When we left the merriment behind—not to mention the kimchi and *bulgogi* (the traditional Korean sesame steak)—we walked away, leaving our new friends in awe of the drinking prowess of the American photographers.

A RISKY TRIP TO THE WALL

The male-bonding ritual that night brought us an unanticipated bonus the next day when our hosts offered to take us on a rare boat ride up the Yalu River to view the remains of the Han Wall along the North Korean side of the river—a trip strictly off-limits to foreigners. Mr. Liu devised a plan to fool any authorities who might catch us in this illegal venture. Kent was to pose as a French engineer (why French is anyone's guess), and I was to pass as a Japanese businessman. In case we were stopped by the police as we made our way to the banks of the Yalu, Kent sat low in the van to hide his six-foot-two frame as best he could, and wore a hat and a hood to cover his face.

We arrived at Linjiang, a small fishing village, where we boarded a boat and took off upstream in drizzling rain. It gave us an eerie feeling to look uphill at the North Korean army fortifications, knowing that sentinels must be watching our every move and have guns trained on our tiny boat.

Because it is illegal in North Korea for any citizen to live within sight of the border, no one was visible on the riverbank. Also, the military is always on the lookout for any defectors who might try to make a swim for China. To this end, the Korean side was cleared of all trees along the riverbank, making it impossible for anyone to approach the river without being noticed.

As we rounded the bend in the Yalu, suddenly the Han Wall was in view. Unlike the mighty Great Wall built by the Ming, it looked like a collapsed counterpart of the rock walls found all over Ireland, and even more so because of the green grass and rainy mist forming its backdrop. It is said that this section of the collective Great Wall, built during the Qin Dynasty, runs all the way to Pyongyang, the capital of North Korea—and someday I would like to be the photographer who gets the chance to see if this is true.

Three short men, or possibly boys, appeared on the bank, beckoning us to shore with shouts and arm-waving. Our guide Liu told us they wanted us to buy their firewood, the only thing they had to trade. The North Koreans would barter for almost any goods from China, perhaps the most coveted being a carton of Chinese (or better yet, American) cigarettes. The men carried primitive-looking bolt-action rifles straight out of a World War II movie.

A small boat manned by three soldiers in ill-fitting uniforms floated by our boat in the opposite direction, and the soldiers ignored us. I couldn't help but think how small and vulnerable those young soldiers seemed, not at all like the aggressive elite troops whom I had photographed on the thirty-eighth parallel, the demilitarized zone between North and South Korea, for another *National Geographic* story; those soldiers had been chosen for their height and size.

Thankfully, there were to be no international incidents on the Yalu on this day. Instead, we toasted our North Korean refugee hosts that evening with a bottle of Great Wall wine and headed south by train.

An off-limits stretch of the Yalu River affords an up-close, if potentially perilous, view of the worn-down eastern Han Wall on the North Korean bank. The wall, built c. 127–130 BC, ran all the way to present-day Pyongyang, the North Korean capital.

山海關

CHINA'S EARLY WALL BUILDERS

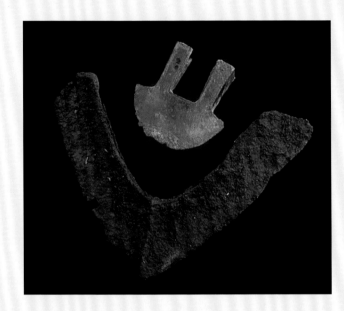

These Iron Age farm implements, a bronze iron hoe and a spade, were unearthed near Xuzhou, China, and date from the Han Dynasty.

In ancient times, the threat posed by Islam and Christianity to the security of Chinese empires paled alongside that from the Xiongnu, Mongols, Manchu, and other barbarian nomads who eked out an existence on the northern steppe bordering China. The respective strengths of the nomads rose and ebbed from 200 BC to the early twentieth century. In fact, non-Chinese invaders from the north ruled China for six of those twenty-two centuries—a testament to the weaknesses inherent in one Chinese method of defense: wall-building.

From the time of the Shang Dynasty (c. 1700–1025 BC), short fortifications encircling even the smallest settlements were seen as necessary by a culture that planted crops and accumulated possessions. Chinese villages were typically located beside rivers and tributaries, which not only provided the water for crops but also for defensive structures. "Walls" were fashioned by digging trenches and piling the excavated earth alongside; the earth was then tamped and formed into ramparts. Channeling water into the trench created a mound-*cum*-moat that protected the village from a variety of real or perceived dangers.

Archaeological investigations have shown that these perfunctory walls provided shelter, sustenance, and safety. Another suggestion that the early Chinese could live safely and comfortably only behind a wall is found in a later pictograph, or early form of Chinese character: *cheng*, which means both "city" and "wall."

Clashes between villages became inevitable. At first, hunters from neighboring settlements competed over the game that would supplement meager grain harvests. Later, groups of villages within a region fought against one another and eventually came under the control of one ruler. Hostilities escalated as numerous proto-states, or kingdoms, arose between the fifth and second centuries BC.

The advent of kingdoms presented new defensive problems. The Chinese had become accustomed to safety behind defensive mounds, but how could a kingdom covering hundreds of square miles be defended? It had been relatively easy for a village leader to enlist a few hundred men as laborers. Now the challenge was to enlist thousands—even tens of thousands—for the task.

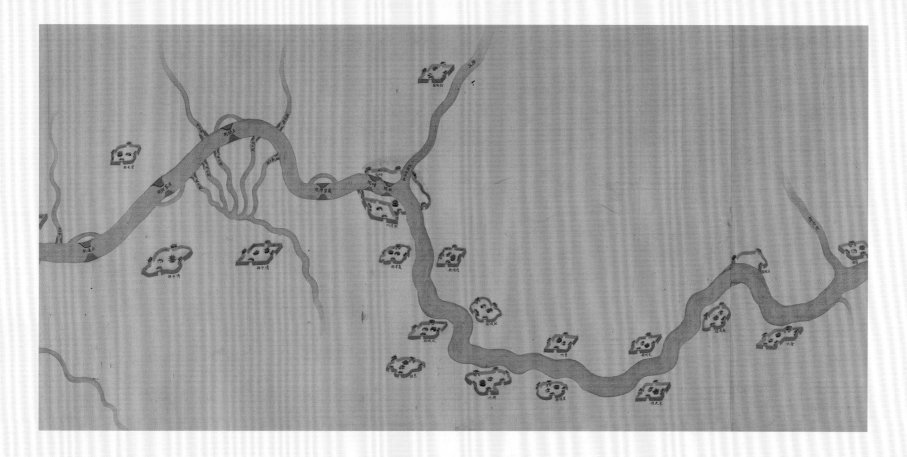

Only during the Iron Age, which arrived in China around the beginning of the sixth century BC, did large-scale wall-building become possible. Modern archaeologists discovered remains of the so-called Wall of the Chu State in what is now central China's Henan Province in 1902. Built in the spring and autumn period of Chinese history (722–481 BC) by the ruler Chu Huiwang, this wall dates from c. 615 BC and probably stretched for more than three hundred miles (400 kilometers). Its construction marked an enormous leap forward not only in building techniques but in weaponry.

The wooden shovels and clumsy stone tools used to create a wall were replaced by new iron tools: sharp and tensile axes for cutting rock, shovels for moving earth, and axles for the easier transport of heavy loads. At the same time, stronger crossbows and

other weapons wrought from iron and steel fed the appetite for clashes among warring kingdoms, in turn leading to the construction of ever more walls to shut out the enemy.

Without such tools and weaponry, the Wall of the Chu State and the great wall built some four hundred years later by the first emperor of a unified China would not occupy a place in the history books. But both were crude predecessors of what was to come—the wall that astonishes the world to this day: The Ming Great Wall that rose in the sixteenth and seventeenth centuries.

The Yellow River is depicted in a detail from a nineteenth-century handscroll, from the collection of the Smithsonian Institution.

在北韓邊界

TWO

SHANHAIGUAN

Where the Great Wall Meets the Sea

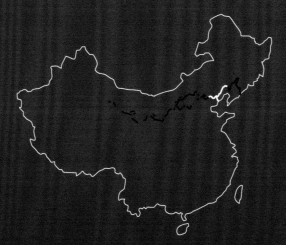

Previous page: Just off the Old Dragon Head portion of the Shanhaiguan Wall, submerged wall rubble is now a reef attracting shellfish—and, in turn, fishermen.

Opposite: Fisherman Zhou Bian Fen slips into a wet suit sewn by his wife before he dives into the waters off Old Dragon Head. His bounty will be crabs caught by hand on the shell beds.

SOME MIGHT ARGUE THAT THE REAL BEGINNING of the Great Wall is at Shanhaiguan, our first stop after exploring the portion of the Han Wall near Dandong, North Korea. Shanhaiguan, whose name means "First Gate Under Heaven," is where the Ming Wall meets the waters of the Bohai Sea. Rebuilt in the 1980s, it looks as one expects the Great Wall to look: massive and formidable, a truly imposing barrier to anyone wanting to get to the other side. Anyone, that is, except the fishermen.

We sat on the beach where the part of the Wall known as Laolongtou ("Old Dragon Head") meets the sea, watching at least a dozen fishing boats circling an area fifty yards offshore. We were too far away for a photograph, so we hired our own boat to investigate. Most of the boats carried shell fishermen dragging nets along the bottom for crabs.

We met Xuan Li Jun, who preferred diving, and his wife, Zhou Bian Fen, who ran the air compressor for their fishing boat. Mr. Xuan wore a homemade wetsuit and used a primitive hookah rig, catching crabs by hand off the shell beds twenty-seven feet below the surface. The couple came here in the late 1980s as laborers contracted to rebuild the magnificent Wall now before us. After the job was finished, they stayed on, looking for work. They ended up as fishermen, working daily in sight of the Wall they had helped build.

The Gate Tower at the First Gate Under Heaven becomes a dramatic backdrop and sounding board for a choir of teachers singing China's national anthem.

Fishing is dangerous work, but life is good nonetheless. The couple makes as much as ¥2,500 ($312) a week, more than seven times the average wage for Chinese wall-builders. The Xuans are modern-day counterparts of the Ming-era laborers who centuries ago were sent to far-flung corners of China to build the Wall. Those workers, like the Xuans, eventually settled there and started a new life.

Our guides told us that it is the remains of the Wall below the surface that make this area especially rich in sea life; the rubble had become the basis for artificial coral reefs. I was glad to witness my first example of the Wall being put to modern good use, in contrast to the Wall's uselessness as a defensive structure five hundred years ago. Even where the Wall stood high and mighty, invaders always seemed to find ways around it, whether by land or by sea.

Later that afternoon, Shanhaiguan also served as a backdrop to some pictures I took of a teachers' choral group practicing for an amateur song contest. The singing was certainly improved by the Wall's acoustics, with voices bouncing off the brick and giving a resonant boost to the teachers' rendition of China's national anthem. Red and yellow hammer-and-sickle flags fluttered in the wind, a fitting splash of color emphasis for the symbol of China.

山海關

THE SUI DYNASTY (589–618 AD)

The meter-high words inscribed above the Shanhaiguan gateway—"First Pass Under Heaven"—resonate with the romance of the Orient. They also mark a portion of the Ming Wall that proclaims "Great Wall" as dramatically as any other. Yet, while it was the Ming who turned this section into one of the most heavily fortified, many historians believe it was constructed atop one of the walls last repaired around 587 AD by the short-lived Sui Dynasty.

During the three centuries after the collapse of the Han Dynasty (206 BC–220 AD), internal strife in a fragmented China led to a cessation of wall-building; resources were rarely available for border defense projects in times of civil war. The Northern Qi Dynasty (550–577 AD) resumed building walls; in fact, the Qi obsessively built separate stretches totaling around 3,300 kilometers in the Shanxi, Hebei, and Henan provinces, from the Yellow River west to the Boahi Sea. The Sui, too, built fervently, but in time their wall-building would do more to undermine the dynasty than to protect it.

Sui Emperor Wen-ti, born Yang Jian, had been a high-ranking official of the Northern Zhou Dynasty, which in 578 AD reunified northern China by defeating the rival northeastern dynasty of the Ch'i. But all was not sweetness and light. Political instability reigned—and when a mentally unstable young emperor ascended to the Zhou throne in 581 after the death of Emperor Xuan, the ambitious and ruthless Yang Jian managed to execute more than sixty Chou princes and to install a six-year-old child as puppet emperor before seizing the throne for himself.

In control of all of northern China, Wen-ti proceeded to assemble colossal armies and establish order within his frontiers. Emulating Qin Shihuang (260–210 BC), the first emperor of China, he embarked on wall-building to keep northern barbarians—in this case, the eastern Turks—under control. Yet Wen-ti's repair of ancient Qin and Han walls in the provinces of Shanxi and Hebei largely served to illustrate how when one route to invasion closes, the enemy finds another. In 582 AD, four hundred thousand archers led by the Turkish chieftan Shetu invaded northern China farther to the west, in Gansu.

長城

秦始皇

姓嬴名政始自始皇乙卯即王位庚辰併天下稱皇帝
在位三十七年居王位二十五年即帝位十二年壽五十

廿

Qin Shihuang, the "first sovereign emperor of Ch'in," undertook to unify China in the third century BC. His massive projects included a national system of roads and a mausoleum guarded by a vast army of terra cotta soldiers, and a precursor to the Great Wall.

Even then, Wen-ti's wall building continued. In 585 he
sent some thirty thousand laborers to the Ordos region
(today's Ningxia and Shaanxi Chinese provinces and
a portion of Inner Mongolia) to build more than three
hundred fifty kilometers of wall. The next year, one
hundred fifty thousand laborers constructed a broken
line of garrison posts on the Inner Mongolian desert,
and in 587 more than a hundred thousand men
labored for twenty days to repair sections of wall, the
locations of which are lost to time.

Meanwhile, Wen-ti began to execute his plan to reunify
the whole of China. He dethroned the puppet governor
of the Northern Chou in 555 AD, and four years later
overwhelmed the last southern dynasty, the Ch'en.
Thus was founded the Sui Dynasty.

Wen-ti had two sons: Yang Yong (the crown prince)
and Yang Guang, whom Wen-ti named as the Prince
of Jin. The accomplishments of the younger son were
impressive even in the dynasty's earliest days. In 589
he commanded the five armies that conquered the
southern Ch'en Dynasty; in 590 he served as governor
of Yangzhou; and in 599 he led the imperial army to
successfully defend the northern border against an
Eastern Turk invasion. His achievements earned him
the title of crown prince when his elder brother was
disgraced after the discovery that he had propositioned
one of Wen-ti's concubines. The cunning Yang Guang
also wasn't above using manipulation to become the
favorite of Wen-ti's four sons. So it was that Yang Guang
became Emperor Yang-ti on the death of his ailing
father in 604—some say, at the favored son's hands.

After Yang-ti took power, his visions of grandeur knew
no bounds. He not only ordered the building of a new
capital city, Luoyang, but also the reconstruction of
the Great Wall built by the Qin and Han—chaotic
projects conducted at such a swift pace that millions
of laborers lost their lives. A Grand Canal dug to link
northern and southern China seemed as much a way
for the emperor to lord his taste for luxury over the
people (his lavish flotilla vessels, all pulled by ropes of
green silk, crowded the canal) as to ease the transport
of provisions between the north and south.

The imperialistic Yang-ti would extend Sui territory
by way of several military expeditions, one of which—
the conquest of a portion of today's Vietnam—saw
thousands of the Sui Dynasty's most formidable
soldiers die after being infected by malaria. But the
most fateful mistake was Yang-ti's invasion of Korea
after tensions flared between the emperor and his
Korean counterpart. A failed foray over the border in
612 AD was followed by another unsuccessful attempt
in 614. Combined with Yang-ti's extremely costly
public works projects (wall-building included), the
invasions of Korea placed burdens on the Sui that
would consume the regime.

In 618, living in fear in southern China in the wake of
famine and civil war that had gripped his northern
homeland, Yang-ti was murdered in his bathhouse by
the son of one of his most trusted generals.

THREE

TO PANJIAKOU
AND BEYOND

*From a Submerged Section of Wall
to a Lofty Running Track*

Previous page: Two portions of Ming Wall (foreground and right) remain visible in the Panjiakou Reservoir, which dates from 1982.

Opposite: Fish traps float on the surface of the fog-enshrouded reservoir. On the far shore, the line of the Ming Wall is barely visible through the mist.

LEAVING SHANHAIGUAN, WE FOLLOWED THE ROUTE of the Ming Wall west, relying on the setting sun as our guide. The Wall undulates over mountains and valleys, between villages and farmland, hidden and revealed without drama or fanfare over the verdant landscape. As we drove along through the lush scenery, we realized we were helping the local farmers with their harvest. Spreading sorghum, soy, and rice on the road to dry, the farmers counted on passing cars and trucks to drive over their crops like mobile threshers, separating the seeds from their stalks.

We followed the Wall until it once again disappeared into water—this time, fresh water: the manmade reservoir of Panjiakou ("Great Wall Beneath Water").

Back in 1982, the Wall was little more to the Chinese than a quarry from which building materials could be cobbled to make houses, more walls, or—as in the case of Panjiakou—a dam to capture and hold the waters of the Luan River. Six years later, all that remained visible of the Wall were two sections, lonely islands in the midst of a vast lake. Flooding forced local farmers to become fishermen, since their villages had been swamped along with the Wall—another modern-day example of peasants adapting to their environment.

長
城

Fishermen anchor their boats over the submerged wall, where fish are more plentiful. The Panjiakou reservoir supplies water to the province of Tianjin.

Overleaf: Two sections of Ming Wall (foreground and center) remain in view at the Panjiakou reservoir. The reservoir was created after the Luan River was dammed in the late 1970s. In times of drought, more wall is exposed as the lake level drops.

From atop the Wall on one of the islands, I photographed a fisherman sculling over a submerged section of the mighty structure. Behind him the Wall emerged, climbing the mountainside once again to dominate the landscape before snaking off into the distance. As I watched him, I wondered how the farmers who lived in a landlocked province miles from the sea—never having been on a boat and never learning to swim—could suddenly adapt to life on a vast lake. But adapt they did. In fact, fishing seems to have been not only more desirable than farming for most but more profitable as well. Today the lake, the numerous fish restaurants in the area, and the Wall itself are an added boon, drawing weekend tourists from Beijing.

到潘家口及周圍

This diagonal stretch of the Huang-yaguan Wall is called Heartbreak Hill by many runners in the Great Wall Marathon. The annual spring-time event has drawn entrants from around the world since it began in the year 2000.

THE GREAT WALL MARATHON

We had little time to reflect on all of this, much less to sample the fare at the floating hotel restaurants dotting the banks of the lake. That's because we had to be at the Huangyaguan section of the Ming Wall for the weekend to photograph the fourth annual running of the Great Wall Marathon, reputed to be the world's toughest.

I was headed for the steepest part of the course—along the two-mile stretch of the Wall with three thousand six hundred steps, rising at more than a forty-five-degree angle, for the best pictures. But rather than the blur of lightning-quick runners I had expected to see, I found what looked more like the Great Wall *walk*; none of the four hundred fifty contestants I saw ran up this dauntingly steep section.

At Huangyaguan, it takes about four hours for the best marathoners to cross the finish line after twenty-six grueling miles, compared to the two hours and change at the Boston or New York marathons. Even with pared-down equipment (just two lenses and two camera bodies), it took me about an hour to make it over this one section. Shooting the Wall was the equivalent of an eight-hour-a-day workout on a Stairmaster, but with steps of varying sizes; some were giants as high as my kneecaps. By the end of this assignment, I was in the best shape of my life!

到潘家口及周圍

Above: Lisbeth Sejers-Neilsen of Denmark takes the 2002 women's crown with a time of 4 hours and 12 minutes. About 9 kilometers (5.6 miles) of the marathon are run on the wall.

Opposite: A marathon runner—or, at this point, walker—gives in to exhaustion near the top of Heartbreak Hill.

NORTHERN QI DYNASTY (550–577 AD)

The Huangyaguan Great Wall we see today—the site of the annual Great Wall Marathon and a handful of museums—was fashioned by the Ming. But they built it atop a wall first erected in the days of the Northern Qi Dynasty and later extended by the Sui (589–618 AD). The Northern Qi were also believed to be the original builders of one of the most visited sections of the Beijing Tourist Wall: Mutianyu, rebuilt by the Ming in the late 1300s, in 1404, and in 1596.

As one of the many short-lived combative dynasties of the so-called Period of Disunity (220–589 AD), the Northern Qi held a minor place in Chinese history. If anything other than wall-building distinguished the dynasty (during its twenty-seven years of rule, millions of laborers were pressed into service to build or repair walls), it was the beastliness of its eccentric founder, Emperor Wenxuan, whose ruthless acts echoed those of Qin Shihuang, the first emperor of China and the first builder of the Great Wall.

Wenxuan, born Gao Yang in 529, grew up with the trappings of power. He was the son of Gao Huan, the most prominent general in the Northern Wei Dynasty's eastern half and the real power behind Northern Wei Emperor Xiaojing.

The Northern Wei dynasty was non-Chinese, founded in 386 AD by the Toba (Tuoba) in what is now Shanxi Province. As the dynasty grew larger and began to control much of the North China Plain, the Toba—a federation made up of Turkic, Xiongnu, and Xianbei tribes—employed an ever-growing number of Chinese as officials and, in the early fourth century, adopted Confucianism and came to resemble a Han Chinese state; a century later, Buddhism came to prevail. Gao Huan (b. 496) would consider himself more Xianbei than Han and resisted following Han traditions—as would his second son and future emperor, Gao Yang.

Gao Yang was actually the least promising of Gao Huan's sons—fearless and decisive yet mentally unstable and awkward. After his father's death in 547 and the assassination of his older brother two years later, Gao Yang consolidated his power, deposed Xiaojing, dissolved the government, and founded the Northern Qi dynasty. The year was 550 AD.

In the earliest days of the dynasty, Wenxuan competently oversaw affairs of state and paid careful attention to the needs of the military; he also had the wisdom to entrust most bureaucratic matters to his prime minister, the efficient Yang Yin. In time, however, Wenxuan's alcoholism, unpredictability, and vicious cruelties would spell the end of the administration of this Son of Heaven, as Chinese emperors were called.

長城

Chinese historian Sima Guang, shown here in a drawing from *Wan Hsiao Tang-Chu Chuang-Hua Chuan*, published in 1921, recounted the colorful and brutal acts of Emperor Wenxuan in his eleventh-century writings.

到潘家口及周圍

At this time in Chinese history, a new emperor was a nervous emperor. In 552, Wenxuan waged battle against the Kumoxi tribe in the Upper Liao River drainage area (in today's Liaoning Province and Inner Mongolia) and successfully secured his northern border. He then built the first portion of the Northern Qi Wall, which ran northward from Lishi (located between the Shanxi city of Taiyuan and the Yellow River) for some two hundred miles (300 kilometers). In the same year, he began to seize cities of the rival Liang Dynasty (502–557), whose kingdom bordered Northern Qi on the south, though no real effort was made to topple the Liang.

In the winter of 553, Wenxuan again led troops into battle after Khitan tribes began attacking the dynasty's northern borders, and he had a personal hand in defeating the enemy. The next year, in the aftermath of an all-out attack on the Shanhu tribe in what is modern Luliang, Wenxuan's cruelty was thrown into sharp relief. After his victory, he decreed that any Shanhu male aged eleven or older be slaughtered, after which all females and younger males were awarded to his soldiers as spoils of war.

In 555, Wenxuan decided that Taoism, a religion developed near the end of the Han Dynasty, should be abolished and absorbed into Buddhism. Yet only after he executed four Taoist monks who objected did the Taoists accept the ruling. The man who dictated that one pacifist religion be merged into the other found it impossible to cease living by the sword.

Wenxuan's militaristic focus resulted in more wall-building, and in the mid-550s more than a million and a half laborers erected four hundred fifty kilometers of wall from Juyongguan westward to Datong. Yet the next threat would come from the south. Border battles with the Liang resumed in 556, complete with assassinations and intrigue.

Wenxuan's behavior grew ever more erratic, his bizarre acts fueled by alcohol. Centuries later, the Chinese historian and statesman Sima Guang (1019–1086 AD) would write in his *Zizhi Tongjian* ("Comprehensive Mirror to Aid in Government") of Wenxuan's strange habits and savagery: "[Emperor Wenxuan] drank heavily and lived immorally, carrying out cruel and barbarous acts at his own whim. Sometimes he sang and danced day and night. Sometimes he spread his hair and wore barbarian clothing with colorful sashes. Sometimes he bared his body and put on makeup . . . He was accustomed to making surprise charges into the nobles' and imperial officials' private residences. Sometimes when it was warm, he would be naked to bask in the sun, but even in the coldest winter, he would strip naked as well and run around. Once, he asked a woman on the street, 'What is the Son of Heaven like?' The woman responded, 'He is so crazy that he really cannot be considered a Son of Heaven.' He beheaded her."

Astonishingly, the drunken Wenxuan's impulse to kill was such that his prime minister Yang Yin took measures to keep the innocent from becoming targets: He put the palace guards in control of a group of condemned prisoners, one of whom would be brought before the homicidal Wenxuan when he had to feed his murderous desires.

Despite his monstrous acts, Wenxuan held onto power in part because he attended to government business and in part because his officials feared the consequences of opposing him. Among the government's priorities was the continuation of defensive wall-building. In 557 the Northern Qi constructed a defense line inside the Great Wall; this secondary wall ran from Shanxi's Pianguan Pass to Xiaguan Pass. A second section, which has long since disappeared, ran from Niangziguan Pass to Huangyangguan Pass.

By this point, Wenxuan's military campaigns had drained the treasury, but in the summer of 559 the dearth of funds did not keep him from taking action against perceived enemies. Suspecting that members of the imperial Yuan clan of the former Northern Wei Dynasty were plotting to take back the throne (Yuan was the Chinese name eventually taken by the Toba founders of Northern Wei), Wenxuan ordered Yuans both young and old to be slaughtered and thrown into the Zhang River.

A month or two later, Wenxuan fell ill and died. Many historians attribute his death to alcoholism, but perhaps the violence rooted deep in his soul was to blame as well. He was succeeded by his eldest son, Gao Yin, who took the throne as Emperor Fei and reigned for only two years (559–560). Fei would be followed by two of the late Wenxuan's brothers: Gao Yan, who became Emperor Xiaozhao (560–61); and Gao Dan, known as Emperor Wucheng (561–65).

Wall-building resumed in 563, when the Götürks, a widely dispersed tribe known to the Chinese as Tujue, threatened to breach the Great Wall in Northern Qi territory and invade. In response, Emperor Wucheng began to extend the Great Wall of the Eastern Wei, a seventy-five-kilometer stretch built in 543, to Yanmenguan Pass; he also saw to it that the inner, or secondary, wall built by Wenxuan in 557 was repaired.

Given Gao family history, it is hardly surprising that all Northern Qi administrations had their share of violence and intrigue. But no Gao leader descended into the madness that caused Wenxuan to bring misery and death to so many.

In contrast, the last emperor—Wucheng's son Gao Wei—would rule wanly over a weakened state as Emperor Houzhou. In 577, the dynasty would fall to the Northern Zhou, one of the many rivals fighting for dominance in a divided China.

到潘家口及周圍

FOUR

BEIJING

The Tourist Wall

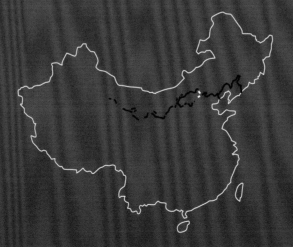

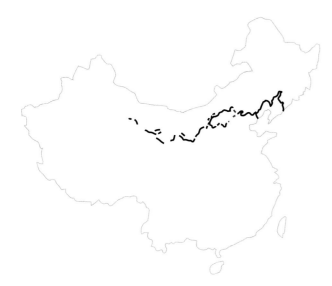

Previous page: Tourists crowd the Badaling Wall, the first section of Ming Wall to be renovated and today the most visited by far.

Opposite: Walking the wall is only one of many activities luring visitors to Badaling, China's most beloved tourist attraction.

ONE BONUS THAT COMES WITH WORKING IN CHINA is the element of surprise. You can do all of the research and gather all of the information possible about one place or another there, but when you arrive, you inevitably find something completely different—and usually far more interesting—from what you ever imagined.

Take the stretches of the Ming Great Wall north of Beijing, which are without doubt China's most popular tourist attraction. I had been to this part of the Wall many times over a twenty-year period, shooting in Juyongguan, Badaling, Mutianyu, and other locations, and I thought I had seen it all. This is where thousands upon thousands of Wall-bound tourists—not to mention visiting American presidents Nixon and Clinton—have been photographed, and because of the so-called Tourist Wall's familiarity I needed to find a new angle. And, as always, China did not disappoint.

長
城

Opposite: Nowhere is the expertise of Ming wall builders more evident than in this section of wall at Badaling. Large stone formations became reinforcements as the builders organically integrated the structure with its surroundings.

Above: With Badaling as her backdrop, a tourist dressed in Ming costume is one of thousands who each week take a trip back in time on the meticulously restored but well-worn wall.

北京

At the Badaling Wall, brilliant fall foliage brings a spot of color to a structure that in some lights is a study in gray. Badaling, the Ming Wall's most renovated and heavily visited section, is roughly five kilometers (three miles) long.

As many times as I'd been to this part of the Wall, I had no idea that it's possible to drive through a wild game park just behind it. A few more miles down the road I discovered a new ski resort, obviously constructed in the *Field of Dreams* spirit of "if you build it, they will come." Nearby were several golf courses, amusement parks and rides, and water toboggans. The Great Wall as a whole is such a tourist magnet that wherever there is Wall there will be a crowd—and where there is a crowd in China, there is business. Sections of the Tourist Wall can even be rented for parties, but the wild game park—Badaling Safari World—may be the ultimate example of charge-ahead development.

Opposite: The athletic and the fashionable flock to the Huaibei International Ski Resort in the Jiugukou natural scenic area. Huaibei, which abuts the Ming Wall (right), is the largest of the five ski resorts in suburban Beijing.

Below: Atop the Jinshanling Wall, Western expatriates mingle before being seated at a wine-tasting dinner sponsored by a California vineyard.

BEIJING MEETS ANCIENT ROME

In a raw spectacle that visitors to Badaling Safari World are unlikely to forget, park rangers toss live chickens to lions at feeding time.

As we approached the game park, the world-famous Wall rose dramatically atop the ridgeline. On the other side was a thirty-foot fence with double moving gates, à la *Jurassic Park*—Badaling Safari World's entrance. Visitors drive their cars into a gated holding area where the first gate closes before the next one in front opens, a system designed to keep the animals inside as the tourists enter and then progress through the park. In the first enclosure, from outside our van, I shot giraffes and zebras with the Wall as a backdrop. This was the perfect photo op, a juxtaposition of animals right off the African plain against the quintessential Chinese landscape.

In the next enclosure were the bears, who were either sleeping or pacing in the demented manner that caged wild animals often exhibit, retracing the same movements over the same area over and over again. But in the third enclosure, I got that jolt of surprise that I have grown to expect on every trip I take to China.

There, in front of our van, was a bus loaded with tourists hanging out of the windows gawking as the safari park rangers tossed live chickens to a pride of hungry lions. And the chickens, it turned out, were only an appetizer. The next animals thrown to the big cats were live sheep. The crowd on the bus cheered like Romans urging on an amphitheater full of gladiators while at least a dozen lions tore into their defenseless prey. Tourists pay ¥30 ($3.75) per chicken and ¥300 ($37.50) per sheep for the privilege of watching the carnage.

The orgy of feeding was one of the most popular attractions along the Wall. I was told that a number of years ago the spectacle took place in an actual amphitheater built for the purpose until a visiting Turkish diplomat, appalled by the slaughter, complained to the authorities in Beijing, who had it shut down.

As I was taking aim at the feeding frenzy with a four-hundred-millimeter lens, the VW Santana I was riding in suddenly jerked forward, ruining my shot. Just as I turned to look at my driver to see what happened, he threw the car into reverse and jerked it back a few feet. That's when I saw that one big female caught up in the frenzy was attacking our van, biting the front bumper while another lioness attacked from the rear.

It was understandable that our driver was throwing the car into forward and reverse gears in a futile attempt to scare off the lionesses, but I shouted at him not to move until I got my picture. The tone of my voice made him dutifully shut off the ignition. I squeezed off a few frames as a chicken flew from the ranger's Jeep to the cheers of the crowd and then disappeared under a crush of lion fur. The van jolted again—and this time I caught sight of a lion biting into the front tire as I framed a shot.

長
城

The peacefulness of the Juyongguan Pass area belies its turbulent early history: it was one of nine vital mountain passes during China's Warring States Period (403–221 BC).

OUR CAR AS PREY

It was all over in a flash, and I slumped back into the seat and quickly rolled up the window; the lions were taking more interest in our black car now that there were no more live animals to devour.

I turned to my driver and could see by the look on his face that he wasn't happy. Both front tires were flat, both bumpers were damaged, and it was obvious the driver was in no mood to further investigate the eating habits of the lions. He was on his cell phone calling for help. Soon, one of our ranger friends came to the rescue, escorting us to the next double-gated area, where we would be able to change tires. But how do you deal with two flats and only one spare tire? We limped toward the exit and left our car overnight at the game park, hitching a ride back to town with some of the park rangers.

They told us that our hair-raising but hilarious incident was a common occurrence here, which explained why each driver had to show his insurance card and sign a release before entering the park. Who could have ever imagined our car being attacked by lions in the shadow of the Wall?

Afterward, I paid our driver two hundred dollars to cover the flat tires and tooth-marked bumpers. But he decided to leave the bite marks as they were—as proof, he said, should anyone suspect that this story was too preposterous to be true.

THE MING WALL OF TODAY (1984–2007 AD)

U.S. President Richard M. Nixon (front, second from right) visited the Great Wall in 1972 as part of his history-making trip to reopen diplomatic ties with China. He is accompanied here by First Lady Patricia Nixon (right) and Secretary of State William P. Rogers (fourth from right).

In the popular imagination, the Ming Dynasty's Great Wall is a magnificent stone structure snaking its way over mountains and across valleys in an unbroken line—and in a few spots on the northern Chinese landscape, this idealized vision is realized. Most everyplace else along the Wall, which once stretched six thousand seven hundred kilometers from seaside Shanhaiguan ("First Pass Under Heaven") westward to arid Jiayuguan ("Last Pass Under Heaven"), the vision is one of decline and fall: In a misfortune of epic proportions, approximately two-thirds of the Ming Wall has disappeared over the past four hundred years.

How could this have come to pass? Sand storms and erosion had much to do with the disintegration, but the more lethal enemy was human neglect and abuse of the Wall from the twentieth century until today. The culprits were vandalism, exploitation, and development, and a tendency for much of the Chinese citizenry of the last century to view the Wall as little more than a relic that long ago outlived its purpose.

When culprits hold sway, the right-minded usually ride to the rescue. In this case, the rescuers whose determination to preserve what is left of the Wall range from the nonprofit International Friends of the Wall to private corporations to Communist Party officials who began to see the potential of the Wall not only as a tourist attraction but as the perfect branding icon for a newly internationalized China.

A hint of the Wall's future was there for all to see when American President Richard M. Nixon visited the Badaling section of the Great Wall on October 23, 1972, during a visit to resume diplomatic relations between China and the United States. Images of a smiling Nixon and his hosts standing on the Wall before a newly restored watchtower were distributed to news outlets worldwide. In ensuing years, a photo session on the Wall became *de rigueur* for visiting world leaders.

It became evident that the Communist government held certain Western habits in high regard. Wall photo ops for the famous paled alongside unbridled development by favored entrepreneurs. In the early 1990s, a combination safari/amusement park had been built next to the Badaling Wall, and the jungle of tourist attractions that sprang up in its wake began to draw increasingly large hordes of tourists.

Modern-day villagers who lived along the Ming Wall stopped taking it for granted only when it promised to bring revenue to townships and individuals. Before, it had been seen as something that could be put to practical use. Stone and sand were plundered for use as building materials, and crops were grown atop some sections of wall. In the eyes of many, the Wall may as well as have risen from the earth as a natural ridge, its history wholly geological.

長
城

This 1907 photograph by Herbert Ponting shows the Wall overgrown and underused. Only in more recent years has this monument been restored, maintained, and become an attraction to visitors from around the world.

北京

Workers rebuild a dilapidated section of the Wall at Huanghuacheng, north of Beijing, in this 2004 photo. Authorities have begun taking steps in recent years to preserve the ancient wall, banning hiking on unrestored sections, and rebuilding parts that have been crumbling.

Also taking a toll on the Wall were two protracted wars. Shanhai Pass and Gubeikou Pass were among the sites bombarded by Japanese forces during the Sino-Japanese War (1931–1945), and hundreds of kilometers of wall were destroyed when Mao Zedong's Communists and Chiang Kai-Shek's Nationalists fought the Chinese Civil War in the 1930s and 1940s. In the latter war, sections of wall were sometimes intentionally dynamited for material to be used for building roads and reservoirs.

As the conflict that would end in a Communist victory dragged on, Mao used the Great Wall as a symbol to rally his supporters. It therefore made sense that, once the new ruling party came to power in December 1949, they would repair some of the damage. Indeed, one thousand three hundred meters of the dilapidated Badaling Wall were repaired in the mid-1950s, setting the stage for later Wall renovations.

In the 1980s, those aforementioned rescuers came on the scene, setting in motion three pivotal events. First, in the fall of 1984 Deng Xiaoping—China's post-Mao de facto leader from the mid 1970s to his death in 1997—launched his "Love Our China, Love Our Great Wall" campaign. As a result, millions of yuan were channeled to the repair of an additional kilometer of the Badaling Wall, which stands some seventy kilometers north of Beijing. The resulting Great Wall Restoration Committee set up by the government began to solicit funds from the Chinese populace and foreigners alike to restore the Wall as a national symbol, and within two years had netted millions. Under the enthusiastic eye of the news media, artists and scholars decorated the wall with paintings, sculptures, and calligraphy that would be sold to raise more funds.

長城

In 1987, the Wall was listed as a UNESCO World Heritage Site, counting it among the most important cultural or natural treasures on the planet. Then, in 1989, International Friends of the Wall—a grassroots organization spearheaded by this book's co-author, William Lindesay, a transplanted Englishman who had studied geography and geology at Liverpool University and fulfilled a lifelong dream in 1986 by running and walking the entire distance of the Ming Wall—began to raise public consciousness of the Wall's endangered status, organize clean-up drives, and solicit corporate donations for wall protection and repair.

The sections of Ming Wall comprising the so-called Beijing Tourist Wall include those at Juyonguan Pass and Gubeilkou Pass and at Badaling, Mutianyu, and Huangcheng. Parts of the Simitai, Jinshanling, and Jiankou walls complete the eight sections of the Tourist Wall, though untouched portions of these walls fall into the "Wild Wall" category.

The most significant repairs have taken place at Badaling and Mutianyu. Badaling, the first section to be opened to tourists and still the most commercialized, is roughly five kilometers long and boasts nineteen watchtowers. Shops and vendors are part of the hurly-burly package here, as are cable cars and fast food outlets. More edifying is the Great Wall of China Museum, which was built on the western side of the Badaling Wall in 1994.

Renovations began on the Mutianyu Wall, just northeast of Badaling, in the late 1980s. The meticulous spiffing-up of Mutianyu is so striking that a December 30, 2006, article in the U.K. newspaper *The Independent* described this section as looking like "something out of the Disney film *Mulan*." The Huanghuacheng Wall in Beijing's northeastern suburbs has undergone two stages of restoration in recent years, and a small portion of the Simitai Wall has also been restored.

Progress in preserving the still-standing Great Wall along its entire length is indicated by the view of the World Monuments Fund: the Fund included the Wall as one of the hundred Most Endangered Sites in 2002 and 2004, but dropped it from the biannual list in 2006. At the same time, in most areas off the beaten path, wall sections deteriorate little by little, risking disappearance either because of their remoteness or a shortage of civil servants who could police the sections and oversee repairs.

If the existing portions of the Great Wall are to survive in their full glory, more than a focus on preservation is required. Vigilance of the most rigorous sort is key, not only in repairing and protecting the Wall from vandals but in holding commercialization at bay. It remains to be seen where the Great Wall's fate lies in a century that may well belong to China—the creator and custodian of perhaps the most intriguing construction ever envisioned by man.

FIVE

THE WILD WALL

Ancient and Untamed

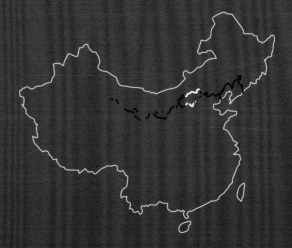

Previous page: The Jiankou Wall in Huairou attests to Ming wall builders' ability to meet the challenge posed by jagged mountain terrain.

Opposite: The Jinshanling Wall runs for about ten kilometers in Ruanping County, north of Beijing, and is the second-longest continuous section of Ming Wall in the east.

THE DIFFICULTY OF PHOTOGRAPHING the tourist-thronged Ming Wall sections around the suburbs of Beijing—the so-called Tourist Wall—doesn't stem from the crowds or the kitschy attractions; both of these are worthy picture subjects. It stems from the closing of the Tourist Wall gates from five p.m. to eight a.m., which means that a photographer is never allowed to shoot in the best light—the golden hour, or the thirty minutes before and after sunrise and sunset.

Still, that didn't keep me from trying. One morning when it was still dark, I jumped over the gates so I could shoot pictures at the Wall. After a hasty run up a few hundred steps to set up my tripod before dawn, I managed an hour's worth of shooting before being escorted out by the guards.

It is that early morning or late afternoon light that makes intact portions of wall extraordinary as the brick takes on a warm glow, changing the gray brick to golden yellow. This was the light I was looking for in 2001 as I made my way toward a more remote and unreconstructed stretch—one of the sections known collectively as the Wild Wall. Left in disrepair for the past three hundred years, these sections of Wall have grown in popularity as a hiking destination for a younger, more adventurous Chinese crowd.

Previous page: The Jiankou Wall is a favorite of the adventurous. Ruined sections on steep inclines have led to injury for more than one intrepid hiker.

Opposite: The Jinshanling Wall exemplifies the Wild Wall through its direct connection to the past— no tourist attractions, no souvenir stands. Its classic views make it a favorite spot for photographers.

MEETING MR. LINDESAY

It was at the Wild Wall that I met William Lindesay—who, along with his band of like-minded "Friends of the Wall," is its self-appointed guardian. (It was Lindesay himself who coined the term "Wild Wall.") Their job is to preserve and protect these dilapidated and neglected sections from becoming future Badaling Safari Worlds. After handing me a headlamp, Lindesay led me up the steep trail behind his farm below the Jiankou section of the Wall for an hour's climb (mostly straight up) in the pitch black of predawn.

Arriving at the top, I had little time to scout the ridge for photographs because the sun was already over the horizon and beauty stretched out in every direction. I worked for the next hour, capturing that glowing brick against dark green and brown backgrounds as the Wall cast its shadow.

A wall section in Simitai shows severe damage to portions of the Wild Wall. While time and the elements have taken their toll for more than four centuries, so too have vandals who plundered stone and other materials at will.

This experience just whetted my appetite for more. Photographers are greedy; they never know when to stop. If you don't see it, you can't shoot it. And if you don't shoot it when you see it, you've missed it.

Wherever there was even a chance for a new angle, I set out to investigate, which meant having to visit all of the Wild Wall from Jinshanling to Simitai, to Huairou and Huanghuacheng. Each section yielded a different picture as a reward for the wear and tear on my ankles and knees. (My first-hand experience has taught me that it's no easier to go down the Wall than to go up; in fact, going down is much harder on the legs.)

野長城

The Simitai Wall, shown here under a dusting of snow, is the most popular section for hiking on the Wild Wall. The walk from Simitai to Jinshanling takes approximately three hours.

Opposite: At the Simitai Wall, a leader of a hiking group trudges along the top of unreconstructed wall. Organized hikes along the Wild Wall are an increasingly popular attraction.

長城

A traveling opera troupe putting on makeup backstage in a makeshift tent theater.

Opposite: In the Hong Lou Temple in Huairou, below the Jiankou Wall, singers in an opera troupe wait to perform. The occasion is a spring festival celebrating Chinese New Year.

長
城

長城

NINE MAGNIFICENT MILES

After seeking out and photographing Wild Wall sections, I decided that, for my money at least, the stretch between Simitai and Jinshanling is the most photogenic. You need a full day to completely appreciate these nine or so miles of Wall studded with switchbacks, steep vertical climbs, and thirty-plus watchtowers to see the effects of the total range of light over the landscape. The bottom-to-top climb alone takes four to five hours at a brisk hiking pace, and that's without stopping to shoot pictures.

We started from the Simitai side at dawn, carrying our camera bags in backpacks because our hands had to be kept free for balance and rock-climbing. A donkey ride took us to below the crest of Simitai, Wanjinglou (Watching Beijing Tower)—at three thousand feet, the highest of Simitai's peaks. They say that on a clear day you can see all the way to Beijing, which is sixty miles away—though with today's pollution that would unfortunately be a very rare day indeed.

野長城

Jinshanling guard houses were constructed with bricks fired in furnaces set up near the building sites. The bricks reinforced earthen ramparts and protected them against the ravages of time.

Overleaf: The Jiankou Wall scales peaks in the foreground and becomes a thin white line on the distant mountaintops.

At this point, I found it unimaginable why an invader would ever even think about attacking the Wall. On the sheer near-vertical drop down the face appropriately named Heavenly Ladder, a climber takes his life in his hands just trying to climb down. One false move could lead to a very serious injury, if not death. Not surprisingly, I chose instead to go the safe though nonetheless painful route down the way I had come up—by donkey.

The rest of the hike toward Jinshanling consists of equally amazing views of the Wall with its numerous towers (I counted thirty-six, spaced roughly every two hundred yards or 180 meters) providing a new perspective around every corner. The nine miles seemed to go quickly, but it was almost sunset by the time we reached Jinshanling for perhaps the most spectacular vista of them all. After we hiked past a few more towers and got above and beyond the Jinshanling Wall exit, the classic Wall shot presented itself: watchtower in foreground, serpentine walls extending from each corner of the frame, and the jagged dragon-backed peaks of Simitai in the far distance— all basking in the glow of the sunset's magic hour.

It was a fitting end to an awe-inspiring day.

野長城

EARLY MING DYNASTY (1368–1449 AD)

The complexities of Great Wall history are compounded by the tendency to assume that the Ming built walls from the time they took power in 1368 AD and to lump the defensive walls of different eras into one mighty structure—metaphorically permissible but physically impossible. For example, construction of the section of "Wild Wall" at Jiankou is more often than not described in literature and on the information super-highway as having been built in the inaugural year of the dynasty's reign, even though the Ming didn't adopt wall-building as a defensive strategy until more than a century later.

Accordingly, it's important to look at the ways the Ming kept the northern invaders in check and why they eventually fell back on the wall-building practiced by their predecessors—the Qin, the Han, and the Sui. Their modus operandi in the first hundred years was not so much to defend the northern border as to set up garrisons from which their northern neighbors could be kept under control, the result of decisions by the first Ming emperor: the rebel leader Zhu Yuanzhang, who took the name Hongwu ("Overwhelming Military Force").

Mongol empire-builder Genghis Khan conquered the Jin empire of northern China in 1211, and by 1215 the Mongols were in firm control of Beijing. The Yüan Dynasty established by Khan would later control all of China under his grandson, Kublai Khan.

By the mid-1300s, a now inept Yüan administration, rivalries among Mongol generals, and open revolt by peasants after disastrous flooding of the Huang and Huai river basins (1351) had destabilized Mongol power in central China and precipitated a revolution. In its aftermath, Zhu Yuanzhang proclaimed the restoration of Han Chinese rule in 1368 with the foundation of the Ming Dynasty and a new imperial capital in Nanjing.

Born to a poor Chinese family during Mongol rule, Zhu Yuanzhang was orphaned at age sixteen, took refuge in a Buddhist temple, and eventually became a monk. Horrified by the temple's sudden destruction by Mongol soldiers, he joined a radical Chinese sect—the Red Turbans, whose purpose was to foment peasant rebellion against Mongol authority. As the cult extended its power and reach, rivalry among its leaders—one of whom was the thirty-six-year-old Zhu Yuanzhang—came into critical play. After a string of resounding victories over his rivals, he became the cult's most powerful leader.

Given his history, it is hardly surprising that the man now called Hongwu took an offensive approach toward repelling foreign incursions. His plan centered on the building of garrisons (permanent military posts) at strategic points in the north. The purpose of these so-called "eight outer garrisons" was to form a base from which to direct Ming influence toward the Mongols. A closer inner line of forts was constructed at Juyong and other mountain passes; it was these forts that would determine the line of the Ming Great Wall that would start taking shape a century later.

永樂

The Yongle Emperor, as depicted in this image from an eighteenth-century album of portraits of Chinese emperors, is sometimes known as the "second founder" of the Ming Dynasty.

His efforts met with success. By the time Hongwu died in 1398, the Ming had established supervision over the Ordos steppe—the Inner Mongolia desert region that was important to the Chinese not only because of its desirability (rivers and lakes in the otherwise extremely arid region made farming possible) but also because of the threats to China posed by nomadic barbarians of the Ordos.

During his reign, Hongwu's policy was "guarding the border with royal blood," meaning he sent his sons north to personally oversee regional defense. He could trust his own offspring, and putting them in charge would also place them on the frontier, where they could contemplate the future of China.

One son was the Prince of Yan—Yan being the area around Dadu (the Mongol's administrative capital), which was renamed Beiping by the Ming. The prince eventually came to power as the Yongle Emperor in 1402, but only after plotting to usurp the throne of the second Ming Emperor, Jianwen (Zhu Yuwen, Hongwu's grandson), whom, for reasons lost to history, Hongwu had chosen as the crown prince.

Yongle wasted no time in asserting his authority. In 1404 he ordered the capital moved from Nanjing to Beiping, which he renamed Beijing ("Northern Capital"). Two years later, he began building a new imperial capital—the Forbidden City.

During his years as the Prince of Yan, Yongle relished the opportunity to lead small armies north from Beiping onto the steppe and engage the Mongols. He captured horses and became convinced that what he had achieved on a small scale could be replicated on a large scale: that a Chinese army could defeat the barbarians and end the frontier threats once and for all. By doing so he would be residing at the heart of his traditional power base and be well supported, though the relocation broke the traditional policy of locating imperial capitals deep in the heart of Chinese territory in order to protect the emperor and the government.

Like his father, Yongle concluded that dynastic security would be strengthened by an aggressive policy toward the protracted border problem—an idea he believed so vehemently that he led five armies from the front to prove it. But the man who would become known as the "Emperor on Horseback" would in time make a fateful mistake: nullifying seven of the eight garrisons established in the steppe by his father.

In the end, Yongle left his successors with a capital that lay just a couple of days' ride from the edge of the steppe and a bitter realization: the nomadic enemy, no matter how small in number, was extremely difficult to defeat. Indeed, future Mongol assaults on Beijing would see relatively unimpeded passage of their armies to the capital.

To correct Yongle's mistake, the Ming would begin to construct their first true wall system some twenty years after the emperor's death. In an effort to protect Han settlers in the Liaotung Peninsula, they built two separate ramparts—each, according to historical records, consisting of two parallel rows of stakes with earth packed between. It was a surprisingly inauspicious beginning for an era of wall-building that would bring about one of the most iconic structures in the world.

The difficult situation in which the Chinese found themselves was hardly black and white. Their tribute system, which dated from the Han Dynasty, benefited the Chinese and foreigners alike by guaranteeing exclusive trade rights to foreign regions. In addition, paying tribute (gifts) supposedly subordinated the foreigners to the Chinese emperor despite the banquets, and entertainments, and gifts the Chinese lavished on the visiting foreigners in return—bestowals that helped them keep the upper hand.

長城

With their "barbarian" northern neighbors, the Chinese tribute system took a divide-and-rule turn, playing one tribe against another and maneuvering their alliances to keep any one tribe from becoming too strong.

It was the tribute system that would be partly responsible for a turn of events that would lead to the building of the Ming Wall. In the 1440s, Esan—the charismatic Oirat (Kalmyk) prince who had united three of the Ordos region's largest tribes under his rule in 1439 and subsequently wiped out the Chinese garrison towns of Datong and Xuanhua—needed to acquire Chinese products to keep the people of the territories he controlled not only united but appeased. Consequently, he began to send annual tribute missions to China, knowing that kowtowing to Chinese authority would net him clothing and foodstuffs for his population in return for products from the steppe—furs and ponies, in the main. But his missions quickly got out of hand, with the products he proffered to the Chinese court growing more extravagant trip by trip and the number of men in each mission growing by leaps and bounds.

Such extravagance placed a burden on the increasingly suspicious Chinese, who had to provide more expensive gifts and entertainments in return. Between 1442 and 1448, Esen sent an average of a thousand men a year to China, and the steppe products they brought with them were usually of questionable quality.

An outright fraud was perpetrated in 1448, when a two-thousand-man mission was claimed by the visitors to number three thousand as a ploy for receiving still more gifts. The outraged Chinese response was to drastically reduce the quantity of presents given.

Needless to say, the Chinese court's decision angered Esen. Adding to his ire was the collapse of what he understood was an agreement that his daughter would be permitted to marry into the Chinese imperial family.

Not one to forgive, the Mongol ruler mobilized forces northwest and northeast of Beijing in the late summer of 1449. Uncertain of how to respond, the twenty-two-year-old emperor Zhu Qizhen (installed as the Zhengtong Emperor in 1435) was swayed by his ambitious former tutor, the eunuch Wang Zhen, to mount an expedition to upbraid Esen.

The callow emperor, Wang Zhen, and half a million soldiers completed a thirteen-day rain-soaked journey to the garrison of Datong, only to find it laid waste by Esen and strewn with Chinese corpses. Wang Zhen chose to abort the expedition, and on the way back to Beijing the army camped at Tumu Fortress.

On September 8, Esen's army attacked the troops and slaughtered the Chinese in what would become known as the Battle of Tumu—a fierce man-to-man clash in which the Chinese had fought valiantly but the Mongols showed no mercy. Among the mortally wounded was Wang Zhen. And the Zhengtong emperor? He was captured but released a year later. Then, after several years, he staged a coup and was briefly returned to the throne.

Yongle's lesson had been learned yet again: Offense was a poor form of defense, and the answer to foreign threats was the resumption of wall-building. Over the next two centuries, the Ming would build walls the likes of which the Chinese had never seen.

野長城

INNER MONGOLIA

Exploring the Qin and Jin Walls

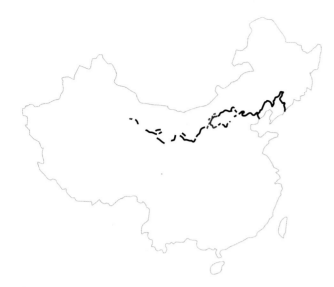

IT WAS NOW SPRING, AND TIME TO CHECK OUT another section of the Wall. I chose to head north into Inner Mongolia, China's autonomous Mongol region, for a look at the country's former enemy and to see what was left of more ancient walls of the Qin and Jin dynasties. We flew to the region's capital city of Hohhot (Mongol for "blue city") and disembarked to find a dramatic change in landscape—rolling grassland that is vast and treeless.

Traveling with me was my favorite fixer from Beijing, Jia Liming. A fixer for a photojournalist is a combination guide-production coordinator-research assistant-interpreter-secretary-accountant-restaurant critic-bag carrier-and sometime driver (in China, though, the driver comes with the car). The best fixers can do it all, and Jia is at the top of their ranks. Once she gets my shoot list of the subjects I'm looking for and the photographs I wish to take, she plans my itinerary and makes all the arrangements, leaving me free to concentrate on my job. Jia's task is to get me to the right place at the right time, and she has yet to disappoint.

We boarded a Toyota Land Cruiser for the drive to Baotou, Inner Mongolia's fastest growing city. Along the way, we were to pass several sections of the Qin and Jin walls—but the former, at Siziwang Qi, wasn't a wall at all. In fact, we couldn't even see it because we were driving on it: the wall was the road.

長
城

Top: The earliest defensive border walls date from the Eastern Zhou Dynasty (770–256 BC) and featured deep trenches to stop charging Mongol horses.

Bottom: Coal powers the giant steel mills of inner Mongolia. Today, many Chinese are lured there by the promise of jobs.

Overleaf: The eroded mound of the Eastern Zhou wall runs right through the middle of the village of Bian Qiang (translation, "border wall"), where its stands six to nine feet tall.

內
蒙
古

An old woman in Bian Qiang put the remains of a wall to practical use, building her house up against, and tunneled into, the ancient Eastern Zhou rampart.

In the twelfth century, the wall built by the Jin Dynasty (1151–1234 AD) was fashioned by laborers who dug a trench and used displaced soil to make a six-foot-high compacted earthen barricade. This trench-*cum*-wall was designed to stop a mounted Mongol's charging horse in its tracks; it was the highest feature on this flat landscape. Now that the wall was worn to just a hump of no more than a foot high after two thousand–plus years of neglect, it made sense to use it as a road, especially in the rainy season when grassland turns to mud. (There wasn't much chance of that happening in 2001, since there had been no substantial rains in this region for about five years.)

I tried my best to photograph the wall road, but failed to make a picture that would compel my editors to run it in the magazine. It looked like what it had become—a rundown, one-track country road.

內
蒙
古

Sitting tall in a Mongolian saddle, a cowboy rounds up horses in Shangdu, once the heart of the Mongol Empire and the site of Kubla Khan's Xanadu.

MONGOL HORSEMEN

At the next stop, the village of Biang Qiang, there was no mistaking the eight-hundred-year-old Jin Wall, which ranges from six to nine feet in height. The residents here are quite proud of the fact that their wall runs right through the middle of town, splitting it in half. In some instances, the Wall serves as the back wall of a house or the front wall of an enclosed compound; in other cases, the Wall stands in as one side of a pen for cows, pigs, or sheep. The villagers use the top of the highest section of Wall, which boasts the best cell phone reception in town, as their primary gathering spot.

Mongolia's fabled horses and horsemen, however, were nowhere to be seen. We were told that because of the severe drought conditions, many horses had died over the winter. Heading farther north, we traveled toward Xanadu, Kublai Khan's fabled summer pleasure palace, now called Shangdu. All that is left there now are the mounds of the city walls in a vast treeless plain, with only a few shepherds watching their sheep pick over the bare ground of the once-great city. Shards of bright green and yellow roof tiles littered the ground, hinting at Shangdu's former splendor.

A shepherd told us about an area family who had two hundred eighty horses that had survived the winter. On visiting the Norbu family ranch, I found the horses grazing the pastures to be scrawny and mangy, but alive. Despite their sorry condition, they would soon be galloping over the hills with Mongolian cowboys in hot pursuit. It was time for the spring roundup.

From the back of a Chinese motorcycle, I used my longest lenses to capture the horses at full gallop, as they dodged and ran to avoid the looped bamboo poles that the tunic-clad cowboys wielded to lasso them. Once roped and caught, the horses were wrestled to the ground by their tails, Mongol-style. A team of wranglers in brocade jackets sat on the frightened horse and administered a dose of modern-day medicine before letting it rejoin the herd. The display of horsemanship I witnessed that morning was enough to explain why the prowess of these northern nomads on the battlefield gained worldwide renown.

Above: For centuries on end, Mongolians have used the same tool to catch wild horses and runaway livestock: the *urga*, a slender wooden pole with a lasso at the end.

Right: A cowboy is resplendent the traditional Mongol horseman's costume. Colorful silk brocade robes are ordinary workday wear for the cowboys, whose horse-tending methods differ little from those of their ancestors.

長
城

Opposite: A girl picks cotton in one of the many fields in the Jinta region, contributing to China's distinction as the world's largest producer of cotton.

Above: In the shadow of the Han Wall on the border between Inner Mongolia and Ningxia, newly harvested red chili peppers are spread out to dry in the sun.

內蒙古

THE QIN DYNASTY (221–206 BC)

Inner Mongolia was the site of a wall built by King Wuling of the Earlier Zhao Dynasty (304–320 BC) to protect against the nomadic horsemen of the northern steppes. Many historians believe this to be one of the three tamped-earth ramparts that would later be transformed into China's first "Great Wall"—the Qin Wall, which some say the Ming would in turn build upon from around 1450 AD onward.

Or did they? The confusion surrounding two walls separated by more than twelve centuries persists even to this day.

What is not in dispute is that the Qin Wall came to symbolize the hubris, grandiosity, and viciousness of the ruler who ordered it built and went on to unite China: Qin Shihuang, its first emperor. Only a man as calculatingly ruthless as Shihuang could force the diverse states of the Yellow, Wei, and Yangtze river basins into one political entity, and at the cost of millions of lives. At the same time, the changes wrought by the Qin in their pre-dynasty years would change China forever. What had been a collection of hereditary fiefdoms would become a bureaucratic government with power invested in a single ruler. The importance of the Qin to Chinese history is further illustrated by the belief that China's very name is derived from "Qin" (pronounced *chin*).

During the Warring States Period (403–221 BC), six states—Zhao, Han, Wei, and Yan in the north and northeast, Qi in the east, Chu in the south—were among those fighting for dominance. But it was the Qin state—which lay westward in what is the contemporary northwestern province of Shaanxi—that would be victorious.

The Qin were considered "non-Chinese" by their rivals because they shared various customs with the nomadic Rong and Di tribes who bordered the Qin state on the west and north. One common custom was a propensity for military adventures. In contrast to the more refined pursuits of the states farther to the east and south, the Qins' compulsion for militarism of the most brutal sort cast them as barbarians in the eyes of their rivals.

The grandson of Qin Dynasty founder Emperor Shaoxian, Qin Shihuang was born Ying Zheng in 260 BC. He ascended to the throne at a mere thirteen years of age and remained under the control of a regent until 238 BC, when as a twenty-one-year-old he orchestrated a palace coup and took full power.

It is said that in the previous twenty-five years the Qin had killed more than a three-quarters of a million soldiers. Hewing to tradition, Shihuang mounted offensives against the states that had yet to succumb to the Qin, whose western topography provided natural defenses and a safe base from which to launch attacks. With the 221 BC defeat of Qi, the last independent Chinese state, the young emperor became ruler of the whole of China.

As early as the fourth century BC, the Qin had discouraged Confucianism—whose worldview was humanistic and benevolent—and instituted Legalism, which saw individuals as inherently wicked and in need of the rule of law. The force behind Legalism was Shang Yang, a skilled official under Duke Xiao (reigned 361–338 BC), the last Qin ruler to hold the title of duke rather than emperor. To facilitate the collection of taxes and the conscription of soldiers and corvée labor (forced labor by government order), every household had been registered.

When Qin Shihuang came to power, his government standardized weights, measures, currency, and script in China for the first time. Yet despite such achievements, Shihuang would earn a permanent place in Chinese history almost as much for his infamy as his innovations. Enraged by what he considered an insult by a Confucian monk—the suggestion that he reinvest the feudal kings—the emperor ordered a statewide book burning, effectively erasing the writings of Confucian historians, philosophers, and poets. Some sources hold that Shihuang also buried hundreds of local Confucians alive, though this claim may be no more than a malicious footnote on the part of early historians determined to dramatize the emperor's cruelty.

Qin Shihuang initiated public building projects on the grandest of scales. For this he relied on general Meng Tian, the descendant of a line of great generals and architects. The vast network of roads built by corvée labor under Meng's supervision amounted to almost seven thousand kilometers of thoroughfares and byways. A canal built to link the Hsiang and Li rivers would, like the roads, facilitate both trade and—should any of the provincials think of revolting—military movement. (As the modernized Ling Canal, the canal is still in use today.) As impressive as these achievements were, the blunt reality is that the work was so grueling—and the demands of the taskmasters so exacting—that millions of men were literally worked to death as they labored to build Shihuang's new China.

Confucius, depicted in this image etched on stone from the Shaanxi Provincial Museum in Xian, founded the philosophy that held sway through large stretches of Chinese history. Confucianism was displaced during the relatively short-lived period of Qin rule.

內蒙古

A view of some of the thousands of terra-cotta warriors unearthed with the opening of Shaoxian's tomb in 1974.

The young emperor had ordered the construction of an elaborate tomb for himself soon after he took the throne, and some seven hundred thousand laborers would work on it for forty years; it is said that many were sealed into the tomb on its completion to ensure that its location and contents remained secret. More than two thousand years later, in 1974, the tomb was opened—revealing, much to the world's astonishment, thousands of exquisite terra cotta warriors. The megalomaniacal emperor who had spilled so much blood uniting China had seen to it that he would be defended for all eternity.

For all of the attention showered on the terra cotta warriors, one second century BC building project would overshadow all others: the construction of the first great wall—or, more precisely, the first "long wall," the term used by the early Chinese.

It was Shihuang's attraction to magic and the occult that precipitated the building of the wall. Around 215 BC he was alarmed by an oracle's prediction that "he who would destroy the Qin is a Hu [northern barbarian]." The emperor quickly ordered Meng Tian to lead three hundred thousand men to rout the Rong and the Di and take control of the territory south of the Yellow River. Meng's job then became to restore and link the three northern defensive walls that had been built by the Zhao, Wei, and earlier Qin.

長
城

Some historians claim that Shihuang's passion for building was so keen that he had Meng tear down the earlier walls and start over. However the Qin Wall took shape, the toll it took on the Chinese people was perhaps even grimmer than that exacted for Shihuang's myriad other undertakings. Labor on harsh desert sands and in rugged mountainous terrain joined with the debilitating effects of bitterly cold winters to take the lives of countless conscripted soldiers, convicts, slaves, and corvée laborers.

The enormity of the job was partly responsible: Though not contiguous, the Qin Wall ran from Lintao (contemporary Minxian County in Gansu Province) to the Liaodong Peninsula (Liaoning Province) and totaled four thousand to five thousand kilometers in length. Describing the Qin Wall in his *Shiji* ("history record"), the venerated scribe Sima Qian (145–190 BC) cited the same route and length: "[The wall] started at Lintao, and extended to Liaodong, reaching a distance of more than ten thousand *li* [around five thousand kilometers]."

Nevertheless, misconceptions abound. The Qin Wall has long been confused with the Ming Wall—the "official" Great Wall built farther south some twelve centuries later. Both ancient and modern sources differ so widely that the question isn't so much whether Shihuang built the first long wall as whether the Ming later rebuilt any sections of it. What is presented as Wall gospel in present-day history books, Chinese Web sites for travelers, and even encyclopedias is too often speculation hardened to "fact."

In 210 BC, the fifty-year-old Qin Shihuang didn't let his declining health keep him from taking an imperial tour of inspection, as he had done many times before. He traveled as far west as Gansu and then east to the Shandong Peninsula, where he climbed Mount Taishan—held sacred by the Chinese because it was the object of imperial pilgrimages from the earliest days of the Zhou Dynasty and beyond. At the same time, age and poor health made him all the more determined to find the secret to eternal life, so Shihuang headed to the peninsula's north coast to receive the wisdom—and perhaps an elixir—from the alchemist Xu Fu, whom he had first met in 219. But this journey would be his last: he fell ill and died before he could return home.

Shihuang was briefly succeeded by his second-born son Huhai, who was too weak-minded to resist the influence of his scheming tutor, a eunuch named Zhao Gao. Together, they wasted no time in exploiting the people even more, raising taxes and conscripting thousands to complete work on the royal palace that Shihuang had begun years before.

Zhao Gao gained complete control before being murdered by Huhai's son Ziyang, who would rule for less than two months. The Chinese people had had enough. Under the leadership of Chen She, a former laborer, they revolted and vanquished the Qin. The victory came almost exactly a year after Shihuang's death.

So it was that the Qin Dynasty, with its paradoxical legacy of unification and unrelenting ruthlessness, died. They were succeeded by the Han, who, after their new day dawned, would have their own long wall to build.

SEVEN

THE LOESS PLATEAU
AND THE YELLOW RIVER BASIN

The Route of the Mongol Armies

Opposite: In the Shanxi Province city of Deshengbu, children play follow the leader. The city, which once housed two thousand Ming soldiers, was one of the many walled forts on the Loess Plateau.

LEAVING MONGOLIA WITH NEW RESPECT FOR ancient China's most formidable enemy, I decided to follow the invasion route that the Mongol armies would have taken in the mid-thirteenth century when Kublai Khan, grandson of Genghis, breached the Jin Wall, conquered the Chinese, and founded the Yüan Dynasty (1271–1368). Taking this route meant that I would travel farther west of Beijing through the rolling hills of the Loess Plateau.

I drove toward Datong, one of the most heavily fortified towns of the Ming defense system (built later as a result of the Mongol invasion), because it was from this direction that most of the attacks were launched. My first stop was Deshengpu, one of the many walled villages studding the Ming Wall, which forms the northern border between Shanxi Province and Inner Mongolia. Deshengpu is one of three forts that stand within a few kilometers of one another.

Children dressed in red, pink, and blue came running, some from atop the wall of this battered five-hundred-year-old Ming village, to check out the foreigner with his camera. The village, which once housed two thousand Ming soldiers, is now home to sixteen hundred poor farmers, some of whom surely are descendants of those fifteenth century warriors. Morning cooking fires fueled by coal created a dense fog over the town. After welcoming us warmly, the children trotted off to school, leaving the town looking deserted.

This "vanishing act" often happens when I'm on assignment: I find a town bustling with people, but where is everyone when the light is good and I'm looking for a picture? Yet once again, photographer's luck was with me.

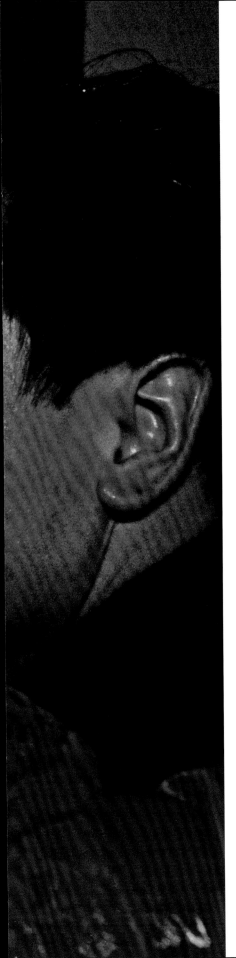

Opposite: On their wedding day in Deshengbu, red-veiled bride Zhu Birong is lifted into the back of a car by groom Lia Yongchun. The Chinese associate the color red with good fortune.

Below: A potato farmer in Deshengbu prepares her seed tubers for planting. Most small farmers in the Loess Plateau hew to tradition, cultivating their crops without the aid of modern machinery.

    A wedding party suddenly appeared, with the groom (whom I later learned was named Liu Yongchun) carrying his bride (Zhu Birong) to a waiting car as a crowd followed behind. I grabbed my cameras and dashed for the car, hoping to get there before the couple. But they were too fast for me. I managed only a pan shot as I backpedaled to get out of his way, capturing the blur of the bride's red-veiled face and wedding gown (red is China's most auspicious color) as she was thrown into the back seat. Yet that was all I needed: the energy of that moment caught on film. With a pleased grin on my face, I moved on to the potato farmers working outside the Wall.

黄土高原及黄河盆地

Above: A cave house dweller stands proudly before the doorway he has decorated with paint and latticework. China's cave houses range from those carved out of town walls to underground dwellings with interiors of brick or tile.

Opposite: The remains of the gates to the walled city of Deshengbu are a wan reminder of the days when it was an important part of the Ming defense system. Today the city is home to poor farming families, many no doubt descended from the soldiers who lived here five centuries ago.

The 400,000-square-kilometer (150,000-square-mile) Loess Plateau is covered with a two-hundred-meter-deep (220-yard-deep) layer of loess—unstratified sandy soil mixed with clay. Terrace farming is the answer to growing crops in this loose soil.

A BOUT WITH DROUGHT

I realized that the wedding was one of the few bright spots for the people of this drought-devastated area. Poor farmers were only getting poorer, with no harvest for the past two years, thanks to almost four years without substantial rains. They planted their potatoes anyway, as they have for generations—perhaps as far back as Ming Dynasty days. The effects of the drought, which began in the mid-nineties, became less drastic in late 2004 with floods caused by heavy snows. Still, many of the farmers were forced to look for work in bigger cities, as most of the sons and daughters had already done. How ironic that the promised land for these Chinese farmers was north of the Wall in Inner Mongolia's mineral rich boomtown of Baotou!

Outside the Wall beyond Deshengpu are arid grasslands, and on the inside is the fertile but fragile Loess Plateau. Loess is the silty soil deposited by the winds that have blown from the deserts to the west over the centuries.

The Loess Plateau extends over three hundred thousand square miles from Shanxi Province to Gansu (the northern part of four provinces). This landscape is uniquely Chinese, found nowhere else in the world: yellow hills often heavily terraced and pockmarked by canyons and gullies where rains have carved away the earth. It is this yellow soil that gives the Huang He, the Yellow River, its characteristic color and name. Frequent windstorms can fill the sky with yellow dust, making it difficult to breathe. The soil is rock-hard when dry but crumbles easily when wet, making erosion a major problem here. Tree-planting projects were sprouting everywhere as we traveled these northern roads.

黄土高原及黄河盆地

Above: Precision plowing, best
performed by humans, is required
for the cultivation of medicinal
herbs in Shanxi.

Opposite: A farmer plows his
terraced fields at dawn on the
Loess Plateau. Most of the plateau
was once covered with dense
forests and lush grasslands, but
vegetation and fertile soil were lost
to deforestation and overgrazing.
In the background the walled city
of Laoying can be seen.

Opposite: A shepherd drives his flock of sheep down a road in Laoying. Many villagers live in cave houses tunneled into the town wall.

Below: Wang Yulian and his wife, Wang Youshen, live in a rock-solid, but poorly ventilated, cave house built into the wall at Laoying.

Overleaf: Outside the walls of Laoying, a farmer unrolls insulation mats on the roof of a hothouse where cucumbers are grown. Hothouse farming is booming in the Loess Plateau.

CAVE HOUSE LIVING

Hongcipu, Juyiangpu, Ninglupu, Pohopu, Shahukou: these garrison towns stand like sentries with the futile task of guarding a border as porous as the ground on which they were built. And things haven't changed much through the centuries, even with no enemies to fight. Villagers come out from behind their walls to tend their fields each morning and return in the evening to the safety and comfort of their homes in walled compounds within the walled villages.

黃土高原及黃河盆地

Opposite: Ice edges a bend of the Yellow River, the cradle of Chinese civilization. Each year, more than a billion tons of mud and silt are swept from the Loess Plateau into the river.

Overleaf: A village that needed no protective wall was Laoniuwan, perched high above the Yellow River. The vertical cliff rising 240 feet above the riverbed safeguarded it from attacks.

I spent a morning in the village of Laoying with Chen Kuan, seventy years old, and his wife Gao Er Mao, sixty-eight, who lived in an exceptionally photogenic "cave house" carved out of a side of the Ming Wall. The brick-faced front looked out on a large walled-in courtyard buzzing with activity. I photographed the couple as they went about their rounds of chores: feeding the pigs, the cow, three sheep, the cat, the dog, the chickens, and the donkey. After fetching water from the town well, Gao disappeared into their cave house to prepare breakfast. Chen lit up his first pipe of the day and extolled the virtues of modern cave-dwelling. Warm in winter and cool in summer, his home cost ¥2,000 (US $250) in 2004, and he proudly told me that it is already worth more. He and his wife couldn't be happier.

The couple invited me to join them for a breakfast of millet gruel, pickles, and rice cakes washed down with thin tea, and as a result I was able to get a closer look at the Wall from the inside. It was a full twenty feet thick at the base, and afforded Gao and Chen a comfortably complete three-room home, with a bedroom, dining/living area, and a kitchen with a foyer. The interior walls were whitewashed and the floor was hard-packed earth. A single bare bulb illuminated each room, supplemented by whatever light streamed in through the window. Chen was right: this kind of shelter made sense in a climate known for its wind-driven, bone-chillingly cold winters and hot, humid summers.

I marveled at these modern "cavemen" and at the fact that more than a hundred million Chinese still choose to live in cave houses. Though Gao and Chen's house was remarkably efficient, one major drawback was a lack of ventilation, though some cave homes in the village had chimneys that protruded from the top of the Wall where soldiers once patrolled.

Gao's hacking cough told me cave-dwelling couldn't be very healthy living. I gave her my bottle of *Nin Jion Pei Pa Koa*, a Chinese herbal cough medicine made with honey and loquat—a remedy I always carry, knowing I'll eventually get a coughing attack if I travel in China for any longer than a few weeks. I gave her instructions to take two tablespoons a day, and also gave her a dozen aspirin (two tablets twice a day). I then left for fresher air on the banks of the Yellow River.

長
城

In the Laoniuwan area, the World Bank funds the planting of trees on the mountainsides above the Yellow River as part of the Green Great Wall project to curb erosion. On the hills in the distance, Chinese characters spell out "Protect the Mother River and Transform the Loess Plateau."

THE GREEN GREAT WALL

Laoniuwen lies in a spectacular setting above a bend in the Yellow River on the Shanxi/Shaanxi border, perched atop a vertical walled outcropping chiseled by centuries of rushing wind and water. (Shanxi and Shaanxi are neighboring provinces, separated in name by a mere additional "a.") Because the two-hundred-forty-foot vertical drop to the riverbed made the village impossible to attack, no walls were needed on three sides. A thirty-foot signal tower stood tall as a sentry, affording an unobstructed view in every direction.

The top of that tower would be my first location here, as I shot pictures of the town looking over walls that normally block the life within from view. But few were stirring at seven a.m. Again I had to wonder, if this was a town of five hundred people, where was everybody? "Out planting trees for the World Bank," I was told.

The villagers were at work on the Green Great Wall—a nine-million-acre project sponsored by the Chinese government and funded by the World Bank. The Green Great Wall is to be a barrier of trees planted across 4,500 kilometers (2,800 miles) of northwest China in an attempt to push back the encroaching desert dunes, much as the Great Wall was built to stem the advance of the Mongol hordes. Typically Chinese in scope, it is the largest ecological project in the history of the world.

Ironically, the Green Great Wall pretty much follows the line of the Ming Great Wall. And, knowing the failure of that Wall to keep out the Mongols (in 1449, the Mongols crushed the Ming army in the Battle of Tumu), the question remains: will the Green Wall be any more successful in holding back the choking sandstorms that descend on Beijing each spring and blanket the city with layers of yellow dust? The Chinese government fervently hopes the answer is affirmative as it looks forward to the start of the 2008 Olympics in Beijing.

黃土高原及黃河盆地

LATER MING DYNASTY (1450–1644 AD)

Above: The Jiayusuan Fortress at the end of the Great Wall on the Hexi Corridor, also known as the Gateway to China.

Opposite: A late Ming tower is depicted in this undated brush and ink image.

After the Ming Dynasty assumed power in 1368, more than a century passed before generals and government officials saw the need to build walls on a large scale. In a few cases, Ming wall-builders made use of the foundations of walls erected by earlier dynasties. For instance, the portion of Ming Wall running eastward from the Liaoning Province village of Laoying to the village of Xiaguan in Shanxi was built on the remains of a wall first put up by the Northern Qi.

Even though the walls the Ming built in the mid to late 1400s included hundreds of beacon towers and sentry posts, the walls themselves were little more than tamped-earth ramparts and trenches forming a continuous line—a barrier built by mounding or gouging the loess soil of the Yellow River Plateau. Only during the last eight decades of their reign, which ended in 1644, did the Ming transform new and existing walls into the magnificent stone and brick structure of today.

The Ming's shocking defeat at the 1449 Battle of Tumu, which saw the Mongols crush the Chinese and capture the Zhengtong Emperor, divided the government into warring factions—Ming officials who urged either offensive or defensive action versus those who favored compromising with the Mongols. What was not in dispute was the Ming military's decline. While earlier nomads' base of operations had been well north of the Chinese border, the Mongols were now moving south to establish settlements in the Yellow River loop. The resulting shrinkage of what had long been a buffer zone reflected both the Mongol's dwindling awe of Chinese military might and a hardening of the Chinese view of the Mongols as barbarians who could no longer be kept in check through diplomacy and trade.

Into the fray walked Yu Zijun, a highly regarded provincial governor who in 1471 recommended to the Ming court that a nine-meter-high wall be built to protect the northwestern Chinese cities. And continuing arguments over how to deal with the northern threat on the part of government officials soon worked in Yu Zijun's favor—ironically, because of a successful military offensive.

In 1472, the experienced general Wang Yue led more than four thousand mounted soldiers to a Mongol stronghold—Red Salt Lake, where the arable land of the Ordos became desert. The Mongols were so soundly defeated by Wang and his horsemen that they retreated farther north. Taking advantage of the temporary break in hostilities, the government gave Yu Zijun what he needed to bring his proposed project to fruition: the command of forty thousand corvée laborers to construct a wall that would run from northeastern Shanxi to northwestern Ningxia—a distance of nine hundred ten kilometers. Work on the wall, complete with beacon towers and several double-layered segments, was finished in three months.

The Ming era saw great advances in the making of porcelain. The firing process was depicted in the decoration of this Ming Dynasty vase, which is housed in the Golestan Palace in Tehran.

A test of the wall's usefulness came in 1482. In a battle between Mongol raiders and Chinese forces led by General Hsu Ning, many enemy soldiers were trapped either against or within the wall and were unable to escape. The victory showed the Chinese people, if not every last government general and minister, that Yu Zijun's wall-building strategy was solid.

In 1485, Yu Zijun began work on the wall built a decade earlier—this one running from near Beijing to the Yellow River, a distance of approximately seven hundred kilometers. This time he delegated the supervision of the construction to other parties. But court politics and intrigue would not only discredit the visionary Yu but also halt the building of the new wall.

Playing a key role was ambitious eunuch Wang Zhi, who had manipulated his way to power by throwing his support behind the warmongering faction of Ming ministers and seeking to enhance his already high standing with the emperor, a lover of warfare himself. Yu Zijun, on the other hand, shared the Confucian belief that eunuchs had no place in court, and in 1484 petitioned the emperor to return them to their original tasks of looking after household affairs. At the same time, Wang Zhi sought to have Yu ousted from the administration.

The scheming eunuch would not have long to wait. When a secretary of the ministry of works inspected the work on the new defensive wall, he reported that the construction was not only too costly but that Yu himself was corrupt. After the eunuchs of the court made much of the report and the Chinese people grew angry, the government ordered work stopped on Yu's second wall.

It would be several decades before the Ming would resume building extensive walls, spurred by the rise of a powerful Mongol leader.

By the 1540s, Altan Khan, founder of the Inner Mongolian city of Hohhot, had restored unity to the steppe. And although Altan sought to resume trade with the Chinese, he was rebuffed. Ming officials also thought it strategic to strengthen fortifications northwest of Beijing near Datong (perilously close to Hohhot), which required, in part, building new walls to connect the crumbling sections built by Yu Zijun.

In 1550 Altan delivered an emphatic message to the Chinese by leading seven hundred men to the weakly fortified area northeast of Beijing, circling the end of the defensive wall, and burning and looting the northern suburbs. Panic spread among the capital's citizens and officials alike.

After Chinese officials told him that they would consider a trade agreement if he were to submit a proposal according to bureaucratic protocol, Altan retreated back to the north. But the agreement never materialized. Instead, as tensions eased, the Ming began to view the Mongols more contemptuously than ever—and in the years to follow, a walled border would announce loud and clear that the days of compromise were over.

So began the construction of the wonder we know today, as the Ming transformed existing tamped-earth ramparts with brick and stone and linked newly built walls with the old. In 1568, the Gubeikuo segment was rebuilt and Mutianyu reinforced, and by the end of the dynasty, the wall would stretch more than seven thousand killometers from Shihuaguan, Simitai, and Juyongguan in the east to the westernmost point at Yumenguan.

Most people associate the Ming Wall with the ancient world, but viewed through the lens of history it is not so old as one might think. In 1571–72, when the Badaling section rose and Jinshanling was reconstructed, Michelangelo's frescoes in the Sistine Chapel had been finished for sixty years, Queen Elizabeth I was entering the fourteenth year of her reign, and the founding of the Jamestown Colony in Virginia was less than forty years away.

The Great Wall was not the only lasting legacy of the Ming: their achievements in literature and painting and ceramics exceeded their bureaucratic and military prowess by far. Yet as inventive as they were, the seeds of their destruction were sown throughout their years of rule.

Those seeds took firm root around 1600, when China—weakened by decades of popular rebellion and a drained treasury—faced a new threat from the north: the Manchu, who had been securing strongholds south of the border. While the Ming were able to hold off the Manchu in battles of the 1620s, the powerful Manchu military commander Nurhaci and his cohorts were cunning plotters, enlisting various Ming officials and generals as advisors. In 1633 the Manchu conquered Inner Mongolia, giving them an easier route to the Chinese interior.

Internal rebellion increased as well. In May 1644, Beijing fell to an army led by the Ming's most prominent rebel leader, Li Zicheng. Only weeks would elapse before the Manchu would crush Li's new government and take control of China.

The Manchu's Qing Dynasty rule of China would span almost three centuries, coming to an end in 1911. From the ruthless Qin emperor who built the first great wall to the Ming who perfected the art of wall-building, the emperors of China would yield their nation to the warring factions of the modern world.

黄土高原及黄河盆地

EIGHT

THE WEST

Along the Silk Road and Beyond

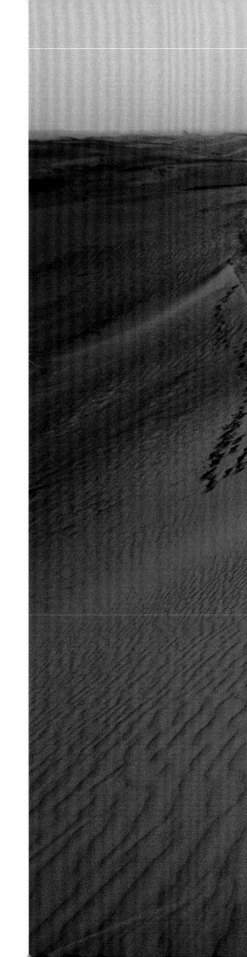

Previous spread: On the Eastern Ningxia/Inner Mongolia border, the longest stretch of unbroken Ming Wall runs for some one hundred kilometers along the Yellow River.

Opposite: The shell of a Han Wall beacon tower stands in stark relief against the sand dunes of Chang-Cheng (Great Wall) County. Much of the wall in this part of Gansu Province is buried beneath the sand.

THE FARTHER WEST WE DROVE, THE DRIER IT BECAME. We passed into Ningxia (like Inner Mongolia, one of China's autonomous regions), where desert reclamation projects date from the 1950s and have seen some success. We were in search of a picture of the Wall disappearing into a sea of sand—the dunes Ningxia is famous for.

I'm often asked how *National Geographic* photographers are able to get great pictures, time after time, story after story. Amateurs often mistakenly assume it's because we have unlimited time to complete our assignments. True, the sixteen weeks allotted for a shoot like the Great Wall sounds generous, especially since the weeks are usually spread out over a year—but on this trip there was little time to waste searching for subjects. I had to cover six thousand miles over almost the entire length of China, all while dealing with variable climatic conditions and a good share of difficult-to-negotiate terrain.

It's at times like these that doing one's homework pays off. Thanks to preliminary research, I knew which pictures I wanted to take even before I laid eyes on the subjects, so the process became less a hit-or-miss proposition and more a hunt for specific quarry.

長
城

The San Guan Gate guarded the most important pass on the border between Mongolia and present-day Ningxia.

Of course, I wouldn't be able to photograph everything I happened upon, so I chose a few representative subjects in each section of the Wall and put them on my shoot list. I then prayed that I'd find my subjects in the right light and the circumstances necessary for a great picture. Thanks to a little photographer's luck, I found those pictures more often than not.

Luck and preparation paid off handsomely in Ningxia, which was justly deserving of its reputation for the best sand dune scenery. I also found and photographed the longest continuous section of the Ming Wall, a sixty-mile stretch which forms the border between Ningxia and Inner Mongolia east of the Yellow River; humps and lumps on a treeless landscape as far as my longest lens could see reminded me of my ten-year-old daughter's fourth-grade drawings of the armored plates on the backs of dinosaurs.

In addition to research and planning, a photographer has to be open to accidental good fortune. The best Wall-and-dune picture I shot wasn't in Ningxia but in Gansu, the next province: Chang Cheng Xiang ("Great Wall Country").

My Beijing fixer, Matthew Hu, had pointed Chang Cheng Xiang out on a map while we were having dinner one evening. It wasn't on our planned itinerary, but how could we pass by a place with a name like Great Wall Country? We detoured off the main road and found that strong winds from only a week before had deposited new layers of sand over the already partially hidden Wall. A beacon tower stood off in the distance, half-buried under waves of sand. We chose our routes carefully as we moved over the pristine dunes so that our footprints wouldn't mar the beauty of the rippled sand.

大西北

The Han Wall runs straight as an arrow on the valley floor near the walled village of Xiakou.

IN THE FOOTSTEPS OF MARCO POLO

The solitude of the sands didn't last for long. As much as I love photographing landscapes, I was eager to visit a few places farther west along China's most famous thoroughfare—the ancient Silk Road, which I had traversed a few years before while following in the footsteps of Marco Polo (born circa 1254, died 1324). This intrepid adventurer, as well as every other traveler along this ancient highway, had to pass through a flat, narrow valley known as the Hexi Corridor, between the Qilian Mountains in the south and the inhospitable Gobi Desert to the north. The wall built by the Han Dynasty follows the same route through this passage.

Marco Polo failed to comment on the Han Wall after he passed through in the late thirteenth century, leading some scholars to seize on this omission to bolster their case that Polo never actually traveled to China. Still, this stretch of Wall is nothing like the massive Ming Wall to the east, and so it's easy to understand why he wouldn't make special mention of such an insignificant structure (ten feet at its tallest), when it paled in comparison to the walls built around most medieval cities—especially the "lofty walls" in the city of Bam in Iran, which he described as at least a hundred feet high.

For the story on Marco Polo (which appeared in the October 2001 issue of *National Geographic*), I had shot the wall to show just how unimpressive it was. Now, I was grateful that my new assignment was giving me the chance to shoot the Han Wall in a different light.

Above: At the end of New Year celebrations comes the Lantern Festival, when celebrants jump over a fire to rid themselves of bad luck. The festival, which dates all the way back to the Han Dynasty, takes place on the fifteenth day of the lunar month.

Opposite: Dressed in traditional spring festival costumes, a group of celebrants from Laozhuang ring in the Chinese New Year, parading from village to village.

Opposite: In the Hexi Corridor, an eroded Han Wall stands out against the backdrop of the Qilian Mountains. This corridor, better known as the Silk Road, is flanked by mighty ranges on both sides.

Overleaf: Ancient meets modern as trucks whiz down a highway that was cut through a stretch of Han Wall near Shandan. Thousands of kilometers of older walls have fallen victim to progress.

Our first glimpse of the Han Wall came outside the city of Wuwei, once a major fortified stop on the Silk Road. I saw it as a curious earthen mound appearing and disappearing alongside the four-lane asphalt highway that the Silk Road has become. When searching for other subjects as I shot the Polo story back in 2000, I'd never bothered to explore the Wall beyond the highway. This time, with the Great Wall as my focus, I could investigate.

We turned a hard right and headed along a dirt track, toward the village of Xiakou, where the Wall seemed to disappear into the mountain. While the village, a former garrison town of seven hundred, was nondescript, this section of Han Wall was magnificent—a good twenty feet high and running straight as an arrow alongside the southern end of town; it then receded into the desert for more miles than the naked eye could follow.

What excited me even more was seeing that the villagers were using the back side of the Wall in their sheep pens, each of which had a hole cut into the Wall so the sheep could be let out to pasture. It's hardly surprising that I was there again the next day at dawn to photograph the shepherds opening the holes in the Wall as part of their morning routine. I took up my position on top of the Wall just before sunrise and caught the sheep jumping and bleating as they passed through holes in the Wall.

One is rarely out of sight of the Han Wall when traveling the Silk Road. Sometimes it's to the right, sometimes to the left, and sometimes the road runs straight through it. And where the Wall runs itself out, beacon towers in the vicinity point the way. These towers were used to send smoke and fire signals to communicate over hundreds of miles, all the way back to Beijing. Today, that function is given over to the cell phone towers dotting the landscape.

Driving the Silk Road meant not having to consult the map or stopping for directions to an obscure piece of Wall. Most of the other roads we had taken ran north to south, so we had only brief glimpses of the Wall, which generally ran east to west. Here along the Silk Road, Route 312 on Chinese maps, I could take pictures just by shooting from the open window of the car. Yan, our steady and reliable driver from Lanzhou, clearly reveled in his newfound freedom of the road, flooring the gas pedal of our Mitsubishi SUV and letting the speedometer climb well above a hundred miles (160 kilometers) per hour. We were at our next destination, Jiayuguan, in no time at all.

大
西
北

Above: For the garrison town of Xiakou, population seven hundred, the wall doubles as the back side of sheep pens, complete with holes through which the sheep can be let out to pasture.

Opposite: Sheep outnumber people in Xiakou, despite the hardscrabble fields the animals graze.